THE WAIT

From the fall of Troy to the Martian sands, and from microwaves to mammograms, *The Wait* is a collection of one hundred poems covering a swelling gyre of human, and sometimes less human, experiences, from previously unpublished poets to established veterans of the literary world.

The profits from the sales of this independently published volume will go entirely to Cancer Research.

***

Camrose Media

EDITED BY
GEORGE SANDIFER-SMITH

First published 2014

Compilation © George Sandifer-Smith. Individual poems are the
copyright of each author as credited. All rights reserved.

ISBN: 978-1-326-03346-0

CONTENTS

CONTENTS

CONTENTS

CONTENTS

Foreword

'What most of us don't realise is that everyone loves poetry.' When Louis Untermeyer said that, poetry was probably more widely read than it is today. More recently, when a well-known journalist said that poetry needed to become accessible and less elitist again, the comments were, for the most part, split squarely between poetry fans saying 'why should we? That sounds like dumbing down,' and non-poetry fans saying 'they can keep it, I don't like poetry anyway'. The schism is wider than ever between those of us who distantly remember poetry as the thing you suffered through the gratuitous analysis of in school, and those of us who kept it up and are cursed to enjoy using words like 'schism'.

Of course, this is nonsense, possibly. Depending on your definition of poetry. People love to share song lyrics over the internet, marvelling at the intricacies of the words. We love a beautiful thing in a bite-sized form, and song lyrics or even short quotes and phrases shared around on social media are just that.

So what about poetry? Why can't that be an acceptable thing to just enjoy? It's partly due to the myth that poetry must be ingested quickly, that it must be understood scientifically within seconds of reading over it quickly. Of course, for those of us who read poetry for pleasure, we know that it's like a delightful meal – you've got to take your time to enjoy it. It's a patient game taking the poem a verse or even a word at a time to get as much as you can out of it. No-one will, or should, laugh at you for misreading it in your own context, because you have every right to interpret it how you want.

Mind you, meeting other poetry fans helps, especially if you take up writing the stuff. For every image of the lonely poet wading through the mists formed from the cold tendrils of a thousand million broken hearts, for every young 'un writing 'Baby, I hate you' (subversion, that, or at least I think that's what teenage me was aiming for), there is a secret to it all; that it is a gift that's far better shared. A way of expressing yourself if you find it more difficult to do so casually. A level of connection based on one of the strongest foundations of human nature, language. The fact that you might end up looking extremely clever in the right circles is quite nice too.

Of course, when lots of poets are featured in one place, you also get that wonderful, terrifying thing – variety. Swift changes of scenery, from the fall of Troy to the present day to other worlds entirely. There's something tremendously pleasing about that collection of so many times and places when it's presented through poetry, or at least I think so. Hopefully you will too.

Anyway, that's enough of my waffle. You're probably reading this after you've read all of the poetry anyway (am I right?). Just a few more words to map out some acknowledgements, then you can get on with reading (or re-reading) the excellent work printed here.

Big shout out to my family, obviously – to Ma, who battled cancer last year and has not only recovered incredibly well, but has written some marvellous poetry (despite never having tried it before). To Pa for staying sane and looking after her through the cancer, the operation, and the subsequent chemotherapy and radiotherapy, and for designing this book. To Mili, who managed to keep her feet on the ground and be a brilliant grown-up throughout the 'Year of the Cancer'. Sharnie Evans deserves a mention (as do her parents, Pauline and Greg) for being so understanding and mature, especially while she went through a Cancer Experience that paralleled my own. Huge great colossal juggernaut of thanks go to Stacey Turner-Williams, who attacked the internet with *The Wait*'s marketing – I would never have made this as good as it is without her. Thanks to the really rather brilliant Anwen Hayward for proofreading the volume. Special mention as well goes to *my* editor, Kathryn Hill, who looked over the 'title track' of this anthology, as she has looked over so much of my work over the years. Obviously, you, the reader, deserve a big thanks for buying this (or whoever bought this for you deserves some credit!) – it's all for an enormously good cause. Last but not least, I'm beyond words (even as a poet) as to how thankful I am for all of the contributors, and everyone who encouraged me to push it this far – from university lecturers to friends to people I barely know who I've met in nightclubs – you're all stars, each and every one of you.

I hope you enjoy *The Wait*.

George Sandifer-Smith,
October 2014

A Crimson Smile

When Spring visits me every year
I pluck his roses
Spring bids me farewell with a fresh green smile.
But this year
when I plucked my roses
Spring bade farewell with a crimson smile
I asked, of course, "What happened?"
He replied, "The stars fell off their perches
They had to look for new orbits
The silver moon was denied her colour,
she wore a purple suit.
The sun shone both as timely and untimely
but swore never to set.
The sea rivalled the tops of mountains
its waves so fierce that
the wind, not to be deterred by land or sky,
allied with thunder and lightning
to burn the lofty trees.
The land was estranged from the feet of dancers then,
but today, it is thrilled by the first
beat and the full swarm of bright flute voices.
The land now opens its heart to receive
the bodies of immortals."

– Faisal Al-Doori

Faisal Al-Doori is a PhD student at Aberystwyth University, originally, from Iraq. His project concerns mysticism in W.B. Yeats' poetry. He is a poet, storywriter, and critic. He has won many literary prizes. He has published many books in Arabic and some articles, poems, and short stories in English.

La Rochelle (Or thereabouts)

Label washed and
re-washed until the print is
gone. Red flakes of it, like rust
flicked away, scattered in the sink.
Partagez un Coca-Cola avec vos amis,
wherever they are.
Fill it with cold water and think of the sea.
Plastic bloats in places
pinched tightly
at the centre
like a Victorian woman. Faint
signs of other languages, now
lost. Indistinct bar codes.
Fill it with sand and think of the sea.
Keep it empty and think of the sea
breeze. Slip it into handbags
and rucksacks. Leave it on train seats
and desks. Find it in your pocket
still tasting sweet.

– Anna Farley

Anna Farley has just finished studying Creative Writing at Aberystwyth University. Her work often attempts to meld something innocuous with an unsettling element. Anna is twenty-one years old and lives in Plymouth.

Third Partner

Never noticed how the time went roping through the dancers
winding through the sides, making links,
pulling partners closer, fraying on cue.
And when did the moon curve into the business?
We stepped into the water and that little disc didn't shatter
and augmented by the static, the music moves the dancers
who, augmented by the silence, move to their partners
and the moon moves too.
My my, right in front of the mountain and the roses,
that shiny looking pair,
sharing words never looked so energetic as that
shiny looking pair sharing words,
out in front of the mountain and the roses.
With
energy to take on the devil and Life itself
out over the mountain, in view of the dancers on the roof,
all pushed and frayed.
If voice is the language of our fathers,
let's write a new field in old grain.

– Jim Kendall

Jim Kendall lives and teaches in the southernmost tip of Italy. He wrote this poem in a cafe for a girl, and has since kept it for himself.

Fy Nghariad

Fy nghariad,
My love.
Like the red, bloodied rose, taking its last breath,
I will die too.
I cannot imagine you dying, like a wilted flower,
Though I know the beauty I see in you will not last
forever.
We have the present, not the past;
The click of the camera, preserved in a photograph.
Rest this necklace on your chest, so I can hear the
beating of your heart.
I am yours and you are mine, entwined on the silver
thread,
because if you are Venus then I am Flora.
So perhaps I can make these roses last a little longer.
For now, however, I shall whisper "Ti yw fy nghariad" -
You are my love
And watch you breathe deeper.

– Shian Streadwick-Augustine-Cain

Shian Streadwick-Augustine-Cain eats a lot of popcorn, writes stuff and collects spoons.

Crabbing

(Scattering my father's ashes on the Wye River,
Chesapeake Bay.)

We go to the river to say goodbye.
We feel your presence, like butterflies grazing our hair.
We feel it in the scent of honeysuckle,
       in the push to be on the river before dawn
with our crab traps.
We feel it in our DNA, in the arches of our feet.
We hear it bouncing down midnight alleys with the
barking of dogs.
We see it in the yellow glow of kitchen screen doors,
       feel it in the beating of ceiling fans window
fans oscillating fans
       that drive out the heat.
We taste what you tasted:
       backyard tomatoes, Silver Queen corn,
Maryland crabs, strawberries,
       and coffee in cups as large as soup tureens.
We feel your presence
in BBQ smoke that stings our eyes when the wind
changes.
And the wind has changed.
It traverses the river to splash over us, making our eyes
tear.

We know you are here,

      swimming in our blood, singing your song

fragments in our ears,

      convoluting our words into crab nets

      so we can scoop out green treasure from the

backwaters

      of the Chesapeake.

Salty

and spicy

and sweet.

– Mary Jacob

Mary Jacob is a poet and Surrealist practitioner. In San Diego, she published and gave poetry readings regularly. Since making Wales her home, she has been active in the arts community, performing poetry, original songs, storytelling, and holding Surrealist games evenings at the Gas Gallery and elsewhere.

Nature In Two Parts

I.

I witnessed the swinging door to nature
square of parallel luscious green,
a robin pirouettes trembling line of washing
curving his flight to a bird feeding crown.
Trotting between dead daisy cups
an ark of paprika leaves
resting on the windows of swollen birch,
the sky a torso in cornflower blue.
His small chest beats like red cedar
robin pops and dances on the lawn,
the tear shaped blossom fell
in colours violet and pierced white.

II.

Door swings open to a front view
seagull beak and red tarred feathers,
spliced on pavements in waves
where metal mounts a scavenger's fight.
A twitching eye lay on sultry tarmac
radish entrails steamed on tyre marks,
engine blurred in chip fat blood
a masked meat in breadcrumbs and gravel.

Curbing and churning looks from young eyes
a canvas of nature's dark colours
pickled and rooted in broken road
soiled beside the clipped and dead hawthorn.

– MJ Duggan

MJ Duggan was born 1971, Bristol UK. He has had many poems published in magazines such as Turbulence, Dwang, Sarasvati, Roundyhouse, Seventh Quarry and many more and is currently working on his second collection '*Notes From A Dystopian Memoir*', and hosts a spoken word evening in Bristol called 'An Evening Of Spoken Indulgence'.

Depression – don't tell me about depression

What's that you say – you feel depressed?
Don't tell me about depression
My depression could wipe the floor with your depression

Depression – did you say you've got depression?
Well, I know how you feel
Ooh! The things I could tell you about depression
Ain't it awful?

I look after my depression – it's important to me
Over the years I've nurtured it – been careful with it
I've even given it a name – Ron – it had to be male!

Yes, I know Ron like the back on my hand
I don't know what I'd do without him
How would I live? What would I do?
I've grown quite fond of my depression
It's safe – I know it – I'd be scared to lose it

I wonder - what would I have if I lost Ron?
Would I lose the other friends I depend upon?
Like my anxiety – that's Gerry
And my OCD – that's Phil
There's a definite pattern of male dependency!

Then the other day I met by chance
A woman who really understands
She told me that she'd been the same
Except her disorders had had a female name

We chatted on for quite a while
And I have to say I admired her style
'Cos although she was serious she seemed quite bubbly
She'd banished her disorders and was feeling…. Jubbly

When I got home I had a row with Ron and Phil and
Gerry
I told them all to pack their bags and move back home
to Cherry
I watched them as they gathered their stuff and waved
'goodbye' as they left
And although on one hand I felt relieved - on the other
I felt bereft

It's been hard going since we split but now I've found
new friends
These fun guys that are moving in are bound to make
amends
The first is Shane – better known as 'Shame'
Next is Dwayne – also known as 'Blame'
Last comes Angus in his kilt

Instantly recognisable and known as 'Guilt'
So you see I'm going to have an exciting life 'cos I'm
clearly on the border
Of something better than depression – it's Complex
Personality Disorder

– Catherine Scott

An unplanned attendance at a poetry workshop sparked a complete change of direction in Catherine Scott's life. With apparent ease she moved from non-judgemental counsellor to confident, opinionated performance poet. Her book, 'A Woman with a View,' published in 2013 coincided neatly with her one woman Edinburgh Fringe show.

The Blackthorn Speaks

Before you lift the shaft
Of your bright blade on the bare bones of my black bark;
Before you come with the craft and crack
Of that cruel axe;
Before you take the cold-hearted hack
Of cheerless haste to chop me down—

Stop. Hold, & heed:

My roots run deep & steep.
Their old fingers, scrabbling & scratching, find treasures
In the filth, redeeming soot & soil
For lustrous pearls of blue-black sloes.
O, bitter they may be; while my spines
Stab out the scarlet sap of your dear blood—

Still. Show mercy:

Let me bloom among the greenwood trees
Another spring, another & another.
Let me unfold from twisted twigs the starry spray—
The foam & spume, white-frothed—of perfect flowers

To crown your head, your brow, though
Gathered, garlanded on such imperfect boughs.

Stand. Do your worst:

Cut my broken branches, if you must,
But let me long outlive you;
For you will surely turn as knotted, contorted, stunted
as I,
Yet full of sweetness in the honeyed heartwood;
So shall I grow to be the prop of your old age,
A thorny shillelagh, if you will—

Stay. I, ancient blackthorn,
Plead for my life.

– Lizzie Ballagher

While Lizzie Ballagher's inspiration comes from the many miles of walking she undertakes each year, her poetry celebrates, explores and maps both external and internal landscapes. Other poets' writing fires her imagination, too: that of Seamus Heaney, Dylan Thomas, Derek Walcott, T S Eliot and Robert Lowell, especially.

Feliz Navidad

*(for Estefania Maria Garcia Poole
lost to breast cancer, February, 2010)*

This was your season; every year,
you made it shine afresh.
Somehow you had a gift for it,
the sparkle and the fuss.
Searching the skies for signs of snow,
you checked your scribbled lists
to trawl the shops in search of gifts
that you would wrap and send
with hand-made cards you crafted
to remember absent friends.

Always they were angel-bright
with jewels like scattered stars,
wishes sent on wings of love
that deepened into prayer.
The peacock card you made
last year is all I'll ever have.
I cannot beg another so
I treasure it the more.

But, late at night,
in the frenzied aisles,

you piled your trolley high:
slabs of meat and chocolate,
bottles of good red wine.
Dates, olives, gleaming veg,
pastries, baskets of fruit;
all you could you bought to feed
and please your 'precious boys'.
Last, you bought Cava, always Cava –
enough to fill a bath.
It had the taste of home, you said,
past laughter, Spanish sun.

For the house, you bought
orchids and fresh green wreaths;
poinsettias, angels in choirs;
dressed your tree with a thousand stars,
decked your table in dreams.
Everywhere sparkle and silver bows,
the smell of food and fun.
You cooked for us
but only cared
to feed us full of love.

This season, though,
you're who knows where
while I make shift alone.

I cannot see an angel
but it brings to mind your smile;
and gifts I've passed
but might have bought
have left me close to tears.
She would have loved
are words that have been
often on my lips.

She would have loved –
and so you did;
that, also, was your gift.
Now your little star
burns sweet and fierce,
a herald in my heart.

– Abigail Wyatt

Abigail Wyatt writes poetry and short fiction. A former teacher at Redruth School, she lives in the shadow of Carn Brea in Cornwall in the company of her singer/songwriter partner, David Rowland, and Percival Dog Esquire. A Pushcart nominee for 2013, her work has appeared in more than eighty magazines. journals and anthologies. She has recently appeared at the Penzance Litfest and the Festival at St Ives. Abigail Wyatt is the author of *Old Soldiers, Old Bones and Other Stories* and one half of *The Fool and the Liar*. She is also the co-editor of the online poetry journal *Poetry24*.

O' Moon Solid Water

Inference recalls
Fawns barrier my romance in poacher's blood
Swollen life red walls
Seeps a splinter doubting the flood

Through the wine mountain
Cradled in insipid graves
I yearn Baptism of prescient
For knighted are the funeral slaves

Outcast and pretend
Your God awaits inside a yard
Measured class and self-denial
Your single life becomes the shard

Cease memory cease to be
O' moon and solid water
Where I'm scarlet warm and alone
She is the devil's daughter

To vex he stumbles over
Mercury seems so close at hand
In a void and dying
He cannot smile, he cannot stand

THE WAIT

Illusion of life scraped unturned
Wild stale endure wild create
White candles melt my windowsill
The midnight walls illuminate

Children milk the river
The wallpaper mocks me like a child
Carpets of wasted-thin cherubs
Keeps my line of salt so wild

– Stewart Alexander

Stewart Alexander is an abstract artist, musician and poet from Wales.

Maladroit

Listen in. The wavelength wanes.
The cause is adamantine, coiled in
russet curls round a limp lace finger,
poised on a pivot of all-imagined splendour
that nestles its weary head in silk.

Intractable the resolution, shaped by cracking
screens and baffled spacemen, running
the dream in bending X-rays round an absent
skeleton, cradled in a closet.

Lipstick slathered inexpertly, mascara mistaken
for eyeliner – what's the difference? – I don't know –
perfumed legs alive, alive and roaring.
There's life in the beast, they tell me:
Don't go too near or it will eat you whole.

I dare.

There's sweat in the carpet and
mirrorballs in your eyes
and a slit in my dress so I can navel-gaze
when out on the town.

I glide on oak (so smooth!) like I'm on
rollerskates at the death of disco, I hear
the synthesiser knell, I feel my balls retract,
I see the lights that topple all the blizzard
windmills wheeling in my milkshake mind and
bell-bottom blurs whirl off like carousels
spinning into the night.

I watch them dance into folkstained fields,
romanticised moors that pull me
back to childhood and snowdrifts
and that sense of wonder easily drawn
from the simples on dandelion drifts
mae'n cariad fy nhadau in a language
I do not know, a borrowed tongue on borrowed time.

Fingers locked, unlocking the sky
on strands astride a tarmac street
that surfeit stands. We are
supine on the sand, we are supine on the sand,
inert to tide, unearthed to shale,
a tempest on the thin blue line that
separates the sea and sky and keeps us here.

Our scansion blows us wide and fishes out
our breath, brief hooks that catch in our teeth

and grit in our gums o spare not me the
lambent waveweaver, spare not me this
shaven monkey's babble, spare not me the
tonguing delinquent rolling in the breeze,

not me,
not me,
not me the wind waker,
the dream sleeper, the sieve keeper,
the drill deeper, the mind quaker, the sooth taker,
the morn intruder breaking bolts of lightning bottles bottling
botching baiting waiting mating sating prating rating
grating dating us,

we dullards supine
on the sand, we tired-eyed achers crying
ourselves all dry and droughts spill out
our irises, our lids close sharp.
Tilt.
Flat.

– Dan Abbot

Dan Abbott has been regularly writing poems and stories since he realised that people might actually read them. He has been published in 2013's Aberystwyth Writing Anthology, *Seafret*, and on the Dead Beats Literary Blog. He is currently writing as the Film Editor for the popular culture website, Surprisingly Competent Media.

Throne

My throne sits abandoned,
once a gilded masterpiece
now faded and scratched.
Paint peels off onto the floor,
a carpet of golden flakes.

The queen who deserted
at the sight of the enemy,
my kingdom lost in cowardice,
trusted by those who believed
I was more than just a pretty face.

My calloused feet disturb the silence,
treading the path
where I once was adored.
Now there is only the cold slap
of my feet against the stone.

The mirror slants off the wall,
a large crack splits the glass
distorting my face.
It's hard to believe that it once
declared me to be a work of art.

My eyes now a dull shade of blue,
my perfect pout puckered,
bones protrude through my paper skin.
Once I filled the whole room,
now I barely leave a shadow.

– Georgie Bird

Georgie Bird is a twenty-five year old Creative Writing and English Literature student at Bath Spa University. She has written poetry since she was a teenager and took a serious interest in it when she started university.

The regency

In the morning, and
Whilst the mountains' zeniths in abeyance
Mime the mosaic clairvoyance
Their glories iterant

Bats are busy flitting across the obscured ether
Heightening the humans' chance – impeccably
Dressed this time – of getting dung-shelled.
Regency holding tentatively on
Until the sun is grown up.

– Opeyemi Joe

Opeyemi Joe is a poet residing in Nigeria, and presently an undergraduate in one of Nigeria's leading tertiary institutions, Obafemi Awolowo University, Ile-ife. He has previously self-published poetry, and his work also has been featured in Lummox magazine, Lost Coast Review, Nebo literary journal, Kalahari review, and the anthology *Breaking the Silence*. He studies Geology.

Passing Times

Her toes draw in the grains of sand,
searching for the memories that slipped through her
fingers

by the sea, she sits

aimlessly tracing the footprints of death
to where caskets are puzzles

life is imagery of emptiness
and cruel humour, a true palace for reinvention of
language

She counts time like rosary,
burying herself to wishes

friends are waves in the ocean,
migratory birds in a season

It rains, it hurts
whenever the wind roars, she is the leaf that falls and
rustles

– Kwabena Agyare Yeboah

Kwabena Agyare Yeboah writes from his home city of Kumasi, in Ghana, where he works as a technical writer. He blogs at www.mragyare.wordpress.com.

This Pen

There is a place
Where men and women live in the shadow of two
walls:

> the wall in whose shadow they work and love
and live

> and the wall that lives in them, whose shadow
they are

and in those twin shadows children are born and
made, are carved out of those

>> shadows, are of those shadows living
>> fragments, and are themselves shadows,

>>> fragments, because they are told they
>>> are, because it is written, because
>>> comfortable men and women have
>>> declared it so, men and women who
>>> are soft, or who if they are hard, are
>>> so by choice, and who know nothing
>>> of those children who are hard
>>> because they know no other way to
>>> be,

>>>> because the hard live and
>>> the soft die.

See here; see this child

(I would have you see him very well)
who is hard as the razor's edge, whose hands hold a
gun more naturally than a book.
See the torn-up olive trees in his face; the skin
hardened by knowledge of
            phosphorous bombs.
            He is the great atrocity: a child who knows
            what a bullet looks like as it rends
                  the flesh, who knows the look of fear
                  in his parents' eyes. A boy who will
                  dig graves before he is a man.

            *   *   *

This pen will dig no graves.
This pen was not at Sabra or Shatila.
This pen had no part in Black September,
            nor was wielded by Leila Khaled, nor by any
other hero.
This pen will write neither peace treaties nor death
warrants;

but they will remember me.

They will carve my name on monuments
            (I fully intend to have monuments)

My words will be tattoos and epigrams.
They will wear my heart on their skin, and call me a
hero,

> I who fought no battles
>
> I who have soft hands
>
> I who could never wear a Semtex waistcoat

They will call me a hero,

> for sitting here,
>
> with my pen and paper,
>
> in safe, safe Aberystwyth.

I assure you, this pen is much less important than you
think it is.

– George Jones

George Jones is a twenty-two year-old writer and musician from Essex, currently living in Aberystwyth, where he is studying for an MA in Creative Writing. His play "The Devil and Molly Malone" won several awards when it was performed by the Broadways Theatre Company in 2013. Jones' music can be found at georgejones1.bandcamp.com.

On Dying in Spring

Flowers flower and buds bud the trees.
It is spring and he is dying of cancer.
Inside his belly, tumours grow like blossoms.
He frosts like winter— hair white, skin pale;
His frame down to bare bones, a skeleton.
In the garden bed, the daffodils rise.

From the hospice bed, he can no longer rise.
Outside his window, wind gusts through the trees
An old tree loses ground - falls down a bare skeleton,
Gnarled and twisted, knots breaking bark like cancer.
With no sun, his skin becomes translucent pale.
It's only outside the window that new life blossoms.

Flowers are brought in, and he smells the blossoms.
Today clouds are thick, the sun reluctant to rise,
The sky rendered grayscale, morning light so pale.
Situated around his hospice bed, we loom still as trees.
Simon and Garfunkel knew it, silence like a cancer
grows, and here I stand - a silent skeleton.

His skin stretches thin, we see down to his skeleton.
Blisters blot his body like connect the dot blossoms.
Friends give last respects, say any words but cancer.

Another night, and in our night sky the moon rise
illuminates the garden, shimmers silvery over trees
Bathes his face by the window, in ethereal pale.

Today he is blue. We flit about him, ghost pale.
The hospice bed supports him, a metal skeleton
the only strong thing in the room. Outside trees
have their spring leaves, bright green blossoms.
We watch each fall for the last, each chest rise
could be the last. Our family becomes a cancer

Mutated through this disease, a living cancer,
A dying cancer, an imitation family so pale.
Outside the sun sets, and in the morning it will rise—
but he will not. He now lays a dormant skeleton.
Friends bring flowers, the air burdened with blossoms.
What remains of him is interred under a copse of trees.

Sheltered by those trees we bid goodbye to cancer.
Under the ground, his body blossoms, bloats pale
skeleton decaying. From his grave, only flowers will
rise.

– Laura Cushing

The Other Side of the Story

Oceans sway, they break white, roll blue

Blue like periwinkle stars, blue like a midsummer night's hues

Blue.

Oceans break on shore carrying human lives

Break, build, break, build, put together a market

Market for our masters. Masters who blister under the sun beneath which we toil

With our callused hands and bent backs as the ocean breaks upon the shores.

I remember a time before we bent to his will

Before we shored up our will, when we roamed the shores at will.

Will we know why we build a market for our masters?

Under the West African sun we cut wood on wood, fit wood to wood

They told us to make a platform

For what reason? No answer.

Oceans roll and break, roll and break

We sweat, toil and break, our wills they break

Our survival is dependent on obedience

Obedience blinded by promises, we go to war against our enemies

Our masters require it.
Bring us your enemies, they said
On the platform you built and -
when your ocean sways and breaks and rolls away
your enemies, your problems will roll away.
We fought, we brought, they bought.
Their promises blinded us to the magic they
wrought.
At first by ones and twos, our people rolled away
Before long we stood on the platforms we built,
tears rolling down our face
With the West African sun setting we were rolled
away - in ships.
Oceans sway and oceans break, ships sway away,
our families break.
The receding sun in the horizon
The other side of our story

– Jasiel Martin-Odoom

Jasiel Martin-Odoom is a Ghanaian poet majoring in Criminal Justice and minoring in Social Justice in St. John's University, Queens, NY. He was born in Ghana and moved to the United States two years ago for college. His poetry is inspired by personal experiences and a desire to share his ideas with the world.

The Girl on the Beach

We watched from the cliff the girl on the beach
As she danced with the waves, now in their reach,
Now skipping backwards on delicate toes,
Keeping the rhythm of the tide's to and fro.
Her sunlit stage sent her outline shimmering,
A feathered phoenix in white flames glimmering.

She raised both her arms towards the sky,
Held up her face, her eyes cast high
To bathe in the sun, her own spotlight,
Offering her dance as one who might
Live forever amidst sand, sky and sea,
Performing her part for the world to see
How perfect she was, this child of Nature,
Full of promise, assured of her future,
That she was at home in this natural beauty,
To answer its rhythms her life's humble duty.

As she gloried in youth, her graceful gestures,
Almost ethereal in their balletic measures,
Her steps barely touched the sun's dappled patches
On the strand where we scattered our daughter's ashes.

– Adrian Rodda

Adrian Rodda, a retired English teacher, and his wife, Lindsay, brought up three daughters in Cornwall and now enjoy life with their five grandchildren. Adrian's verse is often inspired by Cornish folklore and archaeology. In 2010 their daughter, Karen, died, aged thirty-seven, within eight weeks of diagnosis from pancreatic cancer.

Some words

My grandfather one day stepped out for smokes
I think this is how it goes.
He flipped over a scrap of paper,
A house bill or something unnecessary
But still that would be kept.
In a strong hand he writes a sentence;
"Bofus, take care of my girls, Frank."
It was as if he knew.

Thirty years later I'm sifting through paperwork
House bills and receipts my grandparents kept
Dated to more than 10 years before I was born,
Useless now, but important then.
I pick one up, dated October 1979,
And I move to discard it,
It falls to the bottom of the paper bin,
Where it whispers from words
In handwriting I've never seen
"Bofus, take care of my girls, Frank."
A year before he died.

My mother once caught me smoking,
Many years ago.
She said nothing, but the silence of her
disappointment,

Of her fear, tainted the experience for me.
I told myself it was the expense,
Tobacco is a luxury I can't afford.
But then I read those words,
"Bofus, take care of my girls, Frank."
And not only my purse sighs in relief.

My grandfather one day stepped out
To pay for his own death.
I think this is how it goes,
He flipped over a scrap of paper,
And as those thousand monks
For a thousand years
Wrote holy words of dogma
For all those future generations,
In a strong hand he writes a sentence;
"Bofus, take care of my girls, Frank."
And I listen.

– Nej Steer

Nej Steer is a graduate of Aberystwyth University whose adult career plans sometimes get in the way of her childhood dreams of poetic stardom when she eventually grows up. She's inspired by thoughts of legacy and inheritance through stories and memories.

Irreversible Longing

i long
wholeheartedly, constantly, eternally
to run my nimble fingers through your
unraveling system,
to pour a cup of constellations inside your
languid spirit,
to painstakingly swallow
all the lumps forming in your throat,
to serenade sweetly with harmonies your
downtrodden and discouraged eardrums,
to sprinkle my senses through the cracks of the
chasms drilled through your passion,
to plant ideas between the abysmal holes
that thirst for so much as fleeting understanding,
to bellow praise into the gaps of your flesh
that you wish to burn closed.
i long,
oh do i long,
to write you poetry that will portray
even a fraction of your immensely vast soul.

– Patricia P

Patricia P. hails from the Philippines, but she's pretty sure that you can hear her eternal sneezing as far as the North Pole. You can contact her and find more of her work at pennilesspoet.tumblr.com.

Every Woman's Problem at a Summer Fun Fair

The golden coin in the sky
was a proper fireball today.
Feeling like an Eskimo in the desert, I
spent most of the sunlight hours drinking melted ice
with the consequence that now the ball needs to hit
home.
The problem, though, I am not the only one waiting for
her
turn to score a touchdown. I envy the man on my left,
who is
shamelessly giving some freshly pressed apple juice to a
hedge.

– Jennifer Ferreira

Jennifer Ferreira, born and raised in Luxembourg, is of Luxembourgish nationality with Portuguese origins. Jennifer is currently living and studying at the University of Aberystwyth in Wales. Attending and enjoying her second year of English Literature and Creative Writing, she hopes to be a fully-fledged author someday.

THE WAIT

Cases on the central reservation

Seven silent monoliths,
queueing sentinels;
brown, blue, scuffed and battered,
standing side by side in dangerous grass,
waiting.
A crawling cortege
files alongside the raping embrace
of metal strangers;
all eyes away from the cases.
Glances, drawn to glass-strewn,
jagged residue of a careless second
from this snailing train of imposed reverence.

Seven silent wombs,
encapsulators of treasured things;
neatly stacked tee-shirts (freshly washed),
an inflatable dinghy with two patches
clasping last year's beach shoes
in prolonged embrace,
spare cash secreted in white socks,
the postcard list,
two special bedtime cuddlies.

Who will be without a postcard this summer?

Which of the cuddlies is orphaned
along with the expectations and excited intentions
that are broken, scarred,
or ended
here?

Who will claim these seven monuments
to demolished anticipation
after the sirens have faded
into the pastel exhaust
of a "special" weekend?

– Keith Wallis

Keith Wallis is an English poet, an engineering designer bringing an eye for detail into his poetry. He is 'poet in residence' at Ruby Magazine and a moderator at ChristianWriters.com. Though not an academic, he has always enjoyed writing. He began submitting work for publication in the 1980s, after being encouraged by a community writer-in-residence.

Song To The Gods

I'm giving thanks for the wheel
of my astrology; my knees
are seldom needed. I stand up
for science but keep a seat
for sense and sensibility – godfathers
extraordinaire. They have followed
my purpose, cancelled tickets
to raucous concerts that might have
silenced my cymbals. Somehow
I lived while others died. Cancer
means nothing to me, but its opposite
got my goat, dared me to climb
trees, dance in the universal wind.
I belong in no single house,
have sailed the cyclorama.
So thank you for being there,
for saving me from Karaoke.

– Irene Cunningham

Irene Cunningham has lots of poems out in the world: Northwords
Now, Poetry Scotland, New Writing Scotland, Domestic Cherry, and
many more. She hermits herself at Loch Lomond and chats online with
other writers, in this less than perfect world.

Waiting for the theme tune to "Dallas" to start

I don't see skyscrapers or cowboys,
ranches or designer suits.
I see an ice-rink in need of refurbishment
and a girl who's graduated from hired boots,
with blunt blades and collapsed ankles,
to second hand white boots and dresses,
this one a cast-off from an Olympic pair skater,
waiting for the music to start so she can
pivot into a step sequence
hoping that no one is watching
but that someone might see a future for her.

– Emma Lee

Emma Lee's *Mimicking a Snowdrop* is forthcoming from Thynks Press and *Yellow Torchlight and the Blues* is available from Original Plus. She blogs at http://emmalee1.wordpress.com and is a blogger-reviewer for Simon and Schuster. She also reviews for The Journal, Elsewhere, London Grip and Sabotage Review magazines.

Street Santa

Word on the street says now they're hiring men.
Indoors, red suit, hot meals and up-front cash,
enough to score clean needles and a stash;
to guarantee a brief oblivion
from stinks of doorway piss and leaking walls
of cardboard caverns that emerge each night,
rain sodden rookeries, kept out of sight,
of the bright multiverse of festive malls.
But for one neon week enthroned in light,
you are the focus of the make believe.
Excited children's voices interweave,
and thaw the icy glacier of the night,
to make that tinselled till rung wilderness,
a brief escape from white lipped loneliness.

– Don Nixon

Don Nixon has had poems published in magazines and various anthologies , most recently by Offa's Press and Cork O'Bheal. He has won and been shortlisted for a number of poetry and short story prizes. He has work published currently in *Crime After Crime* (Bridge House Publishing) and has released a novel, *Ransom*.

Feline Fate

Cats have nine lives
and nine times kitty thrives
till judgement day arrives

Cats have nine lives
but don't live them sequentially
they run them all concurrently

but even if they didn't
they'd still run out eventually
Cats have nine lives

– John McGlade

John McGlade is a freelance writer from Glasgow. He performs his own poetry, short stories and stand up around the country. He also scripts comedy material for television, radio and theatre productions.

Couldn't Get It Up In Paris

I blame the blancmange.
I blame the restaurants
with their heavy almonds
moored inside my abdomen.
Those sneaky garçons
with suave *accents*
used to covet your loved ones,
sitting upon their stools, waiting to steal our women.

Look at the Eiffel Tower,
standing perpendicular;
a bolt of cold, French blood,
exploding in a discharge of stars.
I blame the River Seine's rimy stream
for skinny dipping screams
and winds that cut like guillotines
through the rosy crack of my wobbling arse.

I blame romance.
I blame *only* France
for the plantation of grapevines
and wines poured into boundless glasses.
Notre Dame's hunchback
smothered his goofy laugh

into an unused mattress
when word got around
    that I couldn't get it up in Paris.

Well, this city is a let-down
(no pun intended).
Mona Lisa is a thumbs-down, a rebound –
the face of Paris represented.
I blame that peacock swagger.
I blame Stella Artois lager.
It's Belgian?
Close enough to be accredited.

It was hardly my fault that I wasn't erected
and had I inspected, or gone exploring,
    I was sure that from inside the hotel room walls,

    I could hear whirring.

– Stephen Watt

Stephen Watt is a poet and performer from Dumbarton whose debut collection *Spit* was published in 2012. Since then, Stephen has won Poetry Rivals Slam, Hughie Healy Memorial Trophy, awards hosted by Tartan Treasures and Federation of Writers Scotland, and recently the StAnza Digital Slam.

Twin (after R. S. Thomas)

Our solemn surface runs free
of stammer, fragile smiles
Absorb every roar of shallow
glances, returned to us in full.
By borrowed aspect, the victimless
thief neither gives or takes away
Seeming scratches that yield no change,
Lines that must earn their age in shade.
Cool to touch, some inimitable fire remains,
a moveable scar of passing consequence;
Surrendered stars, static explosions,
felt-for tears that ceased to drip
Blink room-to-room, as it
was, and might be still.
Sleeping through borrowed sheets
wearing out another soul's relief,
By these silent partners
are ghosts made manifest.
So let eyes grow narrow, near
to dream, where fragments coalesce
And undo the moon of face from
darkness, held close but far away,
To bear no witness at our departure,
a moment paused, mid-sentence, suspended.

– Adam Steiner

Adam Steiner writes about the NHS. His poetry and stories appear in 3:AM, The Cadaverine, Spontaneity, Abridged 0-13, The Literateur, Nostrovia! SquawkBack, NOUS, and the anthology *Poems Underwater*. Adam was selected for the Ó Bhéal Coventry-Cork Twin Cities poetry exchange 2014. He is Deputy Editor of Here Comes Everyone magazine.

Dawn's vixen

Calm, please this eye
of tranquillity that pauses,
questioning. Silent breath, bone dry
taste, bitter, raven's applause.

See the mist, rising, gliding above
to greater heights. Rusted shard, you stand,
brass bold. Beetle juice black beads, caught by doves,
holding all within, ruling over this frozen orb of land.

Cold quintessence, crisp, crackle, tracked
through by you. You who break this
dream held image. White. Frozen, captured, held
in the minds of those who breathe silent, whom others miss.

Your ears face me, I have your attention
fellow stranger, fellow orator. Unknown yet home.
How can thee be borne by his creation?
For thou are too complex, too perfect for his holy tome.

The rusted hue of you appears drawn,
tightened by the ice. Icicle whiskers flicker,
catch the rising, eastern, peaches, thin as cream, dawn.
Wait a while longer, postpone the childish bickering.

I have made you late, dear.
Breaking glance you ebb and flow away,
a lonely voyage back through bramble, alone, senseless fear.
Lost from sight, left alone to battle the day.

A horn sounds.
The thunder of paws.
The day's entertainment has begun.

– Angharad Jenkins Wendon

Angharad Jenkins Wendon's love of writing stemmed from being home educated and experimenting with varying writing styles. She is highly influenced by her surroundings, and recently finished studying for her A Levels. She is about to begin a degree in English and Philosophy at Cardiff University.

The names of things unseen

for Ethan

You discover new spots on our adventures:
Abergele; Deganwy; Prestatyn; Colwyn Bay;
Betws-y-Coed; Llandudno Pier; Conwy Castle.
You and your brothers – pirates and knights –
duelling, peering into dungeons, or racing
to the edge of the jellyfish-dotted sea.

You pack your bag, almost overflowing:
a boomerang; a hacky sack; a water gun
shaped like a shark; an eye-patch and wooden swords,
bunched into place with books; knitting;
paper; pens (for the rainy days)
and a candle, painted in wax with your name.

Your friends teach you bits of an ancient tongue:
trenau; gwylan; "pen; ysgwyddau; coesau; traed",
then you explore my dictionary to find
the names of things unseen, but read, and dreamed –
tylwyth teg, môr-forwyn, coblyn, draig –
wrap words like cowry shells to take back home.

– Kate Garrett

Kate Garrett was born thirtysomething years ago in southwestern Ohio, but moved to the UK in 1999. Her poetry has been published widely, and she is the author of the poetry/flash fiction hybrid *Bewitched* (book six in the Pankhearst Singles Club). She lives in Sheffield, England with her three sons.

* 'trenau ... traed' – train, seagull, "head, shoulders, knees, toes"
* 'tylwyth teg ... draig' – fairy, mermaid, goblin, dragon

Canal Dreams

We met near Telford's
waterway designs, floating
signals as tulips

– David Tallach

David Tallach is a published writer and amateur actor, hoping for a breakthrough with his children's novel. He lives in Inverness, has four undergraduate degrees from the Open University and is about to take a fifth.

In Anatolia

All Turkey cracks
in Saklikent, busfuls
swarm from warm to rock-shade
planks, watering on stilts. We slip
into a froar surprise of stream,
gushed topaz through the gorge.

I smear hot mud on target bitten arms. We
walk against the flow, more and more
find footholds, handle stones, and then
we see there are no fish, no birds, no
one, just purple cliff and us, slip-

sandals, shorts alone in crampon zones. We
turn back, graze slither down to where
people sit, eat bulbul nests, sip
sweetened apple-tea. Webbed
across that shudder-bubbled ground, ducks
present their bills –ekmek –ekmek –
that Turkish word for bread.

– Beth McDonough

Beth McDonough studied Silversmithing at Glasgow School of Art, then an M.Litt at Dundee University. She now works in mixed media, much of her poetry centering around maternity and disability. Her work can be read in Northwords Now, Dundee Writes, Antiphon, Under the Radar, Interpreter's House and more.

Descent

Venerable oak,
mossy knees concealing
roots, deep-delving digits,
winding down through
generations of dust.
Furtive fluttering breaths of breeze,
the languid slip through leaves
of murmured promises;
caressing minds with nagging,
half-glimpsed secrets.
Beneath hoary, ancient arms
a toddler with dirty, digging fingers
squeals with joy, ensnares me.
His beaming dust-streaked face,
expression enigmatic, daring,
laughs and teases me
with my grandfather's eyes.

– Andy Allan

A graduate of the University of Aberdeen, Andy Allan's writing reflects his Highland upbringing and much of his inspiration comes from the natural world and from Celtic myth. His poetry has been published in many small poetry magazines, most recently in, Causeway/Cabhsair, Reach Poetry, Poetry Cornwall, The Dawntreader and The Larcenist.

Trips and Retreats

Disorientated upon a stretch of wood and green,
he grips his notepad in awe.
It is not recycled
unlike the similes of sky
and metaphors for beauty
that the pen feasts upon,
excitement spiralling
across the lines in a drooling blue.
Reciting, he preaches universal harmony,
admiring the taunting and jeering branches crowding,
joking with jagged and stiffened tongues.
The four-wheeled hypocrisy drives them to gossip,
as the wind arrives swiftly with rumours concerning
collections of unread literature
all forged from dead sycamore.
The leaves keep their distance despite the autumnal
drum,
after hearing of the light he refuses to let rest with him
at night.
Branches swing and miss at every opportunity,
as the soil repeats its disgruntled squelch.
Making a turn, he trips;
to the ground's surprise and the forest's delight,
the notepad escapes into the pond

and drowns with dignity.
Reviving himself
he despairs,
noticing his folly
as he retreats towards the car.
Looking around
at those who might have been offended,
he speaks an apology and a promise
without a mouth or pen.
They cannot hear,
yet they quickly accept
and slowly grow to forgive.

– Dean Tsang

Dean Tsang is an aspiring spoken word poet influenced by a mix of button poetry and underground rap. His style ranges from experimental pieces where all the words begin with the same letter to slam poetry rousing people to be optimists. He is currently craving hot chocolate.

Letter

I

You smother your pancakes in serendipity,
licking the maple syrup
from the corner of your lips,
surrounded by
cards and envelopes -
a patchwork of paper
quilting the bed.

Next to your hand,
a last letter
remains unread.

II

At dawn I crept out
so as not to disturb you.
I walked in the woods
where I wandered
alone in the green darkness,
picking bluebells
under the creaking oaks.

In the cool quiet,
I reflected upon
our life together.

III

Upstairs in the bedroom
you're sat up in bed,
rubbing your eyes.

Your hair pours down
drizzling over your ears
clotting in clumps of wild honey,
your cheeks the colour of apples.

IV

I sit by your feet
watching you eat strawberries,
I bought from the market.

The fruit adds a sweet
note to this summery mood;
a subtle fragrance
of vanilla spiked
with bluebells drifts

about the bedroom –
reminding me
of lazy love making –
slow days of summer
the dark scent of earth,
the opium of your womb
spilled from purpled glass
into the soil of my heart.

V

You offer me a strawberry,
dipping its ripened flesh
into a mixture of sugared
cream, spiced with pods.
Reticently, sipping your coffee,
a tired look stealing across your face,
maple syrup
staining your dusky lips:

we kiss.

Here I drown in the embittered
depths of your beauty:
that connoisseur kiss
a blend of smoke and syrup

a woman's perfume;
the breath of frankincense
mingled with mystery.

VI

A new ruby
gleams from your throat
like a blood drop.

The envelope rustles
against the milk of your skin
your fingertips
slipping into its secrecy.

You open the letter
only to throw it back
into a sea of paper –
an ocean of ecstasy
full of dying sighs:
half-whispered words.

VII

Tears stream down from your eyes
as though a waterfall of glistening light

had just lit up your face
as though the sun broke
through the clouds
warming your flesh -
turning the blossom of your cheeks
pink with new life.

The small, hard lump on your breast
is a dark pearl difficult to find

But

the consultant
              thinks
       we've found it

                     in time

                              – Michael Dante

Michael Dante's poetry has appeared in 27 different books and
anthologies. His favourite subjects include Human Rights and
mysticism. He has worked with some of Wales' most innovative writers
and regularly performs his work with the Word Distillery Poets. Also,
he hosts his own show called Chinwag, a writers' open mic that runs
at Aberystwyth Arts Centre, where many award winning novelists and
poets have appeared as special guests.

Watch me stay

The woman with the beautiful spirit
says "I'm not ready to go yet - "
There are too many suns still to watch
More rainstorms to endure
Batches of baked bread still to smell
I'm not ready to go yet;
I have to
Set all the barometers to fair
All Europe's coffees to strong
And all the children to happy.
Also I must Fund the Arts
Right all previous wrongs
Rid the world of warfare and malfeasance.
I cannot go when there are
still too many unkissed faces
and smiles to waken.
There are alarms to unset.
And those frosted ridged brows
and crossed arms -
They all need to be opened.
How can I go
when the ocean has been blackened
and Microsoft have plugged us all in?
Help me stay.

Set my sun to on
The TV to off
My tea to green, wine to red
Then
as the world spins like a dreidel
On the edge of midnight
On the tip of tomorrow
Watch me
stay

– Carolyn Richardson

Carolyn Richardson is a Director of the Scottish Writers Centre, which supports writers living in Scotland who write in all genres, as well as writing in Scots, Gaelic, English and other languages. She is an author and assiduous literary festival-goer. Carolyn taught at the University of Cumbria until 2013 where she supervised PhD Creative Writing students and is an Arts Tutor with the Open University. Carolyn is developing links and writing courses with Montolieu, a French National and International Booktown in the South of France, where she has a holiday villa.

Unconditional

My baby grabs
fistfuls of giant crumpled
poppy freshly burst
from hairy bud -

Dayglo orange lights
dimpled cheeks crashing
into petals larger than
her own rapt face.

Just for now
I don't care how
she rips this newborn
apart – she could
raze every bloom
and I still rejoice
in the perfection
of her wanton hand.

– Rachel Bentham

Rachel Bentham lectures for Bristol University, Bath Spa University
and is currently Royal Literary Fellow at Bath University. She has had
dramas, docudramas and short stories broadcast on BBC Radio 4, and
is currently writing a novel set in steamy nineteenth-century Tahiti.

Why I love the Tanner

I didn't know anything about tanning,
'til I met the tanner.
I didn't know anything about hides,
the gelatine that would be scraped off,
sold to Rowntree's, well it made me think differently,
about the importance I placed on the colours when I
ate fruit pastilles.
I could hear the excitement in his voice
when he was telling me about his pits
the iron ladders in the wells,
the constant use of water with the scum, you can
imagine it
sluiced into the River Hull and out to the Humber.
But it was that nasty smell of lime, it would sometimes
linger on his skin
coming home from that hard day's work.
Well how could I impulsively kiss him?
Sometimes it would be both, coming home wearing
white overalls and black boots
I used to wonder was he working in a mortuary.
More excitement in his voice as he told me
he'd been up at the rendering plants,
drying fat from bone and protein, and we are having
chips in lard tonight!

I did try to show great interest, a very worthy and
respectable job
but rendering too,
surely it has to be thought of as one of the dirtiest jobs.

– Johanna Boal

Johanna Boal is married with three grown-up children, and lives in
Beverley, East Yorkshire. She works as a librarian and in her spare
time loves to read and write. She has been published in magazines,
showcased online, shortlisted in poetry competitions, and recently had
a poetry pamphlet published by Poetry Space, Bristol.

Thunderstorm At Georgioupolis 15.9.05

The air is made of metal.
Up in the mountains a blind god stumbles.
Summer is now on another channel.
All around us the afternoon crumbles.

Afterwards
out over the Aegean
lightning continues to torture the clouds
in a mad white experiment.

– Ian Mole

Ian Mole comes from Sunderland, but has lived in London for over forty years, apart from spells working in Australia, Greece, Poland and Argentina. He currently works as a teacher of English to overseas students and conducts music-based tours of London.

Mammogram

Despite the chill of a February morning,
a man with waxy orange skin is outside
the clinic hooked up to a mobile drip, smoking.

Can you put on the gown please, not catwalk style
but dry like wax paper or butterfly ash.
Then three rounds of the harsh machine.

On the way home purple crocuses, alive
in the crusty, snow-blanched soil. And I wondered
what kind of flower would I choose, in the end.

– Rona Fitzgerald

Rona Fitzgerald was born in Dublin and has been living in Glasgow for nineteen years. She is a member of the Federation of Writers (Scotland). Her poems have been published in the Dublin based Stinging Fly in July 2011, and a number of anthologies published by New Voices Press.

Brutus of Troy

How often have we heard · of Hector and of Troy,
Of Achilles, soft-ankled, · and Aeneas, Aphrodite's son.
Such songs of sorrow · scholars tell, but seldom sing
Of Brutus, from Iulus born, · and his brother Corineus:
A bond of battle, · not of blood.
From Ilion[1] his fathers came · to fairest Italy and
founded
Alba Longa. There Ascanius[2] · in almighty majesty
Sat in splendour, · as a king.
Against his puissance · none prevailed,
Nor any foe, for fear, · would his forces face.
Now Brutus daily · went to butts,[3]
Loosing arrow after arrow, · his aim was famed,
And in the chase · he chased away the days.
But fickle Fate for him · had planned his father's fall.
Fabled Iulus one day · for the forest made
Upon his steed · to see his noble son.
Alack, though, Brutus by mischance · mistook that
mightiest of men.
A stag he saw, · and so his shot was swift.
His shaft struck heart · but not the hart he wished:
A dead deer he did not find, · rather his father dear.
He was cast, for patricide, · from his patrimony,
Upon the waves · from Italy he wandered wide.

In his sojourn sought he · some sanctuary for his soul:
Though Africa and Asia · at last he came to Attica.[4]
There met he men from Ilion · and married fair
Ignone,
Daughter of the Grecian King. · But he did disapprove;
So far · they flew again.
He liberated those lost Trojans · to be hailed their
leader.
Upon a desert Isle Diana, · in a dream, displayed their
destiny:
A western island · in a western sea.
Here Corineus · comes into this lay:
A Trojan he was too · and Trojans led
Upon the banks of Gaul. · Thence Brutus came
With his warriors, · wishing no more to wander.
To French Aquitaine · these new friends
Went and hunted · in the woods.
The Pictavian king · sent parley to find peace
With these strange soldiers · stranded on his shores.
The ambassadors approached · and to Corineus asked:
"Whence come ye · and whither go?
Why do you chase · in this Kingly copse?
Goffarius the Great · has given you no leave to game."
Corineus replied: · "We could not ask
When no one was · within our view."
To his insolence · Imbertus, an ambassador,

Answered Corineus · with an arrow.

But this shaft he sidestepped · and struck Imbertus

With his bow in hand, · breaking his head.

The embassy unto · their king escaped.

To answer this assault · he an army raised

To answer blood · with blood. Now Brutus

Sends the women · to the ships, and soldiers

Calls to challenge · the Gallic King

Who was in arms · arrayed against him.

The forces · faced their foes,

And with sword and spear · and deadly shafts

A battle fought. · Now Corineus in the fray

After many hours · saw both sides holding still:

Neither one · could overcome the other.

So he rallied his men · and with his right wing

Charged into the centre · causing such carnage

That the French · were put to flight.

Corineus chased alone · the cowards from the field,

"See how many fly · for fear of but one man!"

Brutus of his brother said, · their battle won.

But some, such as Subardus, · were not so easily
subdued.

He struck at Corineus, · but was slain. His stand
though

Threatened to renew the battle, · so Brutus

Charged to Corineus, · and together chased

Their enemy again, · their overthrow achieved.
Goffarius, defeated, · summoned other Gallic Kings,
And all agreed · to rid Aquitaine of Ascanius' son.
The Trojans then perceived · that they could not
prevail,
So went to find · their fated home
Across the sea. · And after sailing
Found that blessed isle of Albion · which Brutus
humbly named for himself,
And called it Britain, · while Corineus claimed
Cornwall
As his own, · to which his name he gave, again.
A festival they held · where they had first set foot upon
the shore,
To praise the gods. · But giants who
Inhabited that isle · detested these invaders,
And took up arms · against the Trojans in Totnes.[5]
But against these mighty giants · the men of Troy were
mightier yet,
Brutus himself slew many · with his shafts.
The Trojans threw down · triumphally their foe,
Save the greatest of the giants · named Gogmagog.
He challenged Corineus · to fight in single combat.
The two grappled together · the giant seeming
To get the better, · battering the son of Troy,
Breaking his ribs in sunder · and was stood to slay

The Trojan who had · tumbled to the earth.
But Corineus summoned · all his strength,
Charged at the giant · and pushed him off the cliffs.
In the frothing flood · the giant was felled.
Brutus then became · the first of Britain's Kings,
Lord of one united isle, · united evermore.
New Troy he founded · on the Thames,
Trinovantum, London was, · and Trinovantes all his
people;
And not only Kings · come from that Kingly line,
But all Britons · still bear Brutus' blood.

– Jonty Brawn

1. Another name for Troy.
2. Iulus.
3. An archery field.
4. In Greece.
5. The site of their landing.

Jonty Brawn, aged twenty-one, is a fourth year Classical Studies student
at the University of Edinburgh. Born in Surrey, raised in Cornwall, and
educated at Monkton Combe School, he takes most of his literary
inspiration from Anglo-Saxon literature.

Litchfield last looney poem

Friends, where do they come from?
How did they know so quick?
That the old gals felt quite poorly
And is in fact well bloody sick

I know that ive got Cancer
You cant dress that up or down
And ive watched Holby City
When they pull the curtains round

The kindness of the doctors
To have to do the task
To tell you that you'll pop your clogs
And that these months will be your last

We all know that were going to die
We've known that from the first
So don't feel sad or cry for me
My life has been a blast

With happy times and laughter
Some heartache and some tears
But they are just a measure
To calculate the years

Of friends that you have gathered
To help you with your tears
To help your near and dear ones
Come to terms with grief and fear

Then i will have lived with laughter
And my life will be complete
This poem may not flow too well
Coz im feeling rather beat
But its the last one you will ever get
Good luck now, be inspired
Looney Litchfield is closing down
I think ive just retired

– Janet Litchfield

Her name was Janet Litchfield and she lived in an English village called Stevington. She had two sons and three granddaughters who adored her. She taught them all about art, poetry and appreciating nature which is why this is such a good way to remember her.

Poem kindly submitted by Ciara Litchfield.

For Women Who Travel The West Highland Line

Do not alight at Corrour
unless you wish to change.
This is a station without a town,
no taxis, no buses.
Waiting permitted, short stay or long.
Luggage set down, emotional,
not for reclaim.

Step down lightly at Corrour.
For here in the middle
is a beginning, an end.
A wilderness of dream
where you seem to see,
but do not comprehend
quite the lie of this land.

And while the train, line-tethered,
moves on, you stand
with your hand shielding
the future immense.
Turn slowly around
for your choice in a sense
is a radius, a time to be found.

– Linda Henderson

Linda Henderson lives in Skye and writes as a way of learning her cultural landscape there. In 2002 she graduated from the Strathclyde/Glasgow Creative Writing Masters course. Linda's work has been published in many journals, including, most recently, Words from an Island and Gutter 10. She is a cancer survivor.

Absinthe

Your eyes are the colour of absinthe
and I am the flame
balanced above the glass of you
as my heart's greasy machinery
sniggers in the dark.

Valves are clocked into military
position, cogs are swallowed
into my spine like stars.

The wires within me
have always been tripped to detonate
my heart's grenade-like charm
has threatened many.

In your tipsy presence now
dressed in billboards and shadows
secondary fires blaze in my abdomen,
a thermal wave envelopes my body
like a tidal wave crystallising salt.

My heart rattles at hypersonic speed
fragments of dying love
pierce me from the inside out.

With each sculpted heart comes
a suicide vest
we finger the remote
controls in our sleep.

– Janette Ayachi

Janette Ayachi (b.1982-) is a London-born poet who graduated from Edinburgh University with an MSc in Creative Writing. She has been published in over fifty journals and anthologies; shortlisted for a few prizes, winner of The Barbara Burford Prize from The Young Enigma Awards 2014, is the editor of an online arts journal, *The Undertow Review,* and author of poetry collections *Pauses at Zebra Crossings* and *A Choir of Ghosts.*

Where is the good in goodbye?

Goodbye, goodbye, it's a lexical sword,
A semantic, a symbol, a boring old word.

Yet when I watch you drive away,
It becomes almost impossible for me to say.

One kind kiss before we part,
Though we separate, you are still in my heart.

We only part to meet again,
It's only a question of where and when.

Keep our time of absence sweet,
Shortly in the hope to meet.

To say hello takes a minute of our time,
Forever it takes us to say goodbye.

The worst thing seems to be this sweet farewell,
A gut-wrenching affair, on which we don't like to dwell.

These tears and sighs simply make me ask why,
Where is the good in these sodding goodbyes?

– Claire Wiggins

Claire Wiggins is a recently qualified English teacher. She completed her literature degree and teacher training in West Wales and will be starting her career there. She is an avid reader and enjoys writing poetry in her spare time.

Deer on Highway 9

It is Halloween.
I wear the black velvet dress,
scoop neck rimmed with black-purple ribbon,
and short tight sleeves that,
as I sit in the rocking chair,
cuts off circulation in my arms,
that hang with a flab,
my body loose
like a strange disease,
or exercise - lack of,
catching up with me.

Do I want to go to the Halloween party
of my very cool friend Kathleen,
who is present,
welcoming me with delight,
as if she sees who
I never show, and no one cares to know,
her fingers' phalanxes carving in the air, hips turning
forward, backward -
telling of dreams, art, dark Celtic Samhain.

I lie on my bed.
I don't feel like being around strangers,
when I feel numb.

"Let me greet you like Kathleen might, let me be with
you,"
I say.
"I want to see you, really be with you."
I open myself to myself.

I am afraid
of when and how and will my husband will go
and I am sad.

This has been a distant neighbor, this wistfulness,
one I haven't visited,
I have felt like nothing,
but then I couldn't feel much,
being a stranger.
Even this sadness isn't mine,
I can't trust it yet, or can I?
Can I?
I 've gone on, strong,
not losing control
like I did at the hospital
sobbing on the nursing station telephone
to my shocked sister,
after asking the surgeon
where the cancer spread.

Or like Rose did
crying "I don't want to lose him!"
when I tucked her in,
when we got back from the hospital.
She hadn't visited.

I'm tempted to say no one would want to see me
as I am now
but let it be said,
I see myself tonight.
I lie in my bed with cats - one cuddling between my
legs, another by my head.
One kneads my back, I am afraid he'll tear velvet,
it may be worth it, but his nails hurt, so I turn
 to my side.

It is so quiet in the pine bed with the acorn top
 and the flannel sheet.
Daughter and husband gone trick or treating.

I hear
language I don't know well,
I didn't learn at home,
Not Yiddish, yelling, blaming,
But "Painese."
It is six months, no - a year, of painese,
that I never speak.

It is such a quiet
agony,
a slight rolling of inner eyes, a sigh.
I didn't know.
As I open my eyes
I see there are four cats tucked in around me.

Airing out like spring cleaning in a musty hotel
a relief, a sigh,
and I think of going to Kathleen's Halloween party,
freeways away in West Hills.

It's Halloween,
and soon it will be Christmas
when he was diagnosed last year.
(We got the biggest tree, even two trees,
a pine and redwood).
Now it's the CAT scan,
soon it may be the PET scan
or the surgery to reverse
the ileostomy.
And he plugs on,
afraid?
And he is tired.
And he hasn't written for
so long.

He is himself
when he writes,
as if he's lit a pipe,
though he never did smoke a pipe,
but his soul lights
like when he sat by the fire,
Logan, West Virginia.
I've seen a picture of him in the snow,
his moustache and snow in front of a barn.
And I was there, when we got engaged,
red and yellow leaves fringing
from the wooden lacquered kitchen table,
black stove to the side,
walls, light rock lined with books,
sitting by the wood burning fireplace in the living
room,
the house made of rocks, he and his twin brother
cemented,
near hills and hollers I saw him climb like a goat.
The Mountain Call magazine he co-founded,
in stacks in the closet.
The patchwork quilts made by the neighbours, on the
bunk-beds.

I drink in the quiet like good music.
I hear sputters, candle flickers.

Rose is back.
She is as lively about Halloween
as John and I are quiet about our fears.
She says, "You have to see my bowl of candy,
you won't believe it."
The styrofoam bowl, a tortilla warmer,
is brimming with round and shining wrappers of every
lumpy size.
She says, "It must be a day invented for dentists."

I don't want to go dead again for anything.

I've seen this look I feel in the support group,
in the round, frank face of Dar,
like the look of the deer that night, on Highway 9 in
Felton,
the thud, and the crack of the shiny fender on antlers,
my headlights, running into the redwood forest,
pulling over, looking for him.
No one knows what it is, her home.
But that pain is on her face. She lives with it.

– Claudia Gold

Claudia Gold is creator of ShameIntoJoy.com, "Healing Story-Time"
tele-sharing, and the upcoming "Senior [in the} Moment" radio show,
and book *The Rabbi of Las Vegas*. Her deep adventure is to help herself
and others be whole, heart-enriched and well-nourished through being
a writer, mom, Baha'i, mystic, dancer, social worker and educator.

Euston Station

The station is full of pocket-sized conversations,
of people arriving and reluctantly parting,
of emotions surfacing on their travel-lined faces.
I compare their noses as they embrace and find
comfort in each small likeness while clinging
to each word you say like a limpet on a proud aging
ship,
just as I did so many times

when I was little enough to sit in the crook between
your feet and your legs
as you explained the workings of Nipkow disks and
space flights decades before my existence,
and as dreamers we hung in that moment,
we who can only see the light from other galaxies
through telescopes on clear dark nights
and speculate on the wonders of
humanity's humble accidental accomplishments.
We share this deep in our marrow.
These stretched minutes waiting at a station with you
are gold dust.

It was that close to leaving us without you. Tears pinch
and stop up my throat. That dark other place
without you there,
tugging my life packed into one bag
alone amidst the connections.

I mean to tell you that I will take you someday on
holiday
somewhere where we can look at stars
but my platform number is already up
and we are forced by the onward tide
of rolling suitcases to make a hasty goodbye
amidst the bodies of people like us
without as much as an "I love you".
I've left a piece of my heart in you
to keep safe
until my return.

– Heather J C McLean

Heather J C McLean is a London-born human being studying for her PhD in English Literature at Aberystwyth University. Her research examines lesbian identities and relationships in twentieth century fiction. She enjoys creating things from yarn, long walks, cheesecake, gaming, and dabbling in creative writing.

I See Heaven

I want you to be my guardian.
Occasionally grandparents can become protectors
and you have the advantage.
While we are stuck on earth with calloused feet
from putting too much pressure on ourselves,
yours are creamy and smooth.
Wings let you choose to walk or fly,
to talk amidst the clouds or make them cry.
I want you to be my guardian angel.
I know it won't hold up in court,
but it holds up in my heart.
If the pearly gates are any indication,
I'd say you were a class A lifer.
My corporeal body is not made for wings,
so don't worry about the stitching.
My wings are duck feathers,
flying south for the winter.
I want you to be my sunny skies,
my refuge in the eyes of God.
You're my guardian angel;
I'm just a sinner.

But every time I write,
I see you.
Every time I write,
I see Heaven.

– Jocelyn Mosman

Jocelyn Mosman is a student at Mount Holyoke College in Massachusetts. She has been writing for over a decade, and has recently published her second volume of poetry, *Soul Painting*. She is interested in international human rights law and writing on an international level.

M.I.A.

We fought our own wars among the roses;
Wooden swords as weapons
against the demons of growing old.
He traded it all in,
for the real thing.
His flannel shirt for a Kevlar vest.
A saucepan for a helm.
He wanted a greater game.
His own blood was not enough.
My big brother had gotten braver,
when I wasn't looking.
My big brother had gotten older too.
For the first time in my life,
I'm old enough to understand.
It is fear I see in my mother's face,
As she waits on the words of a stranger.
And I wait for my brother by the back door
In my old, broken trainers,
with a wooden sword.

– Bethany Shepherd

Bethany Shepherd was born with a pen in her hand. From quiet beginnings in a small East Midland town to her literature student life at Aberystwyth University in Wales; writing has always been involved. Poetry or prose, her pen won't leave the paper until parents or publishers take it away.

Cannoli

I take a picture
of a woman taking a picture
       of a man sitting in a wheelchair
       at an Italian restaurant.
She takes the picture not
because he's in a wheelchair
       but because he looks like her
       father looks - or looked, before
the shaky signatures of Parkinson's
began. A ring pierces the accordion
       music playing on the loudspeakers.
       The ring is of a pleasant ringtone
but it's ugly, somehow.
A seven minute phone call tells
       her that it's all over.
       A patron drops a forkful of
cannoli onto the marble floor,
and the woman walks out. So do I.
       I get home and put the image onto
       my desktop. I open the file, full
screen, close it, and drag it to the trash.

       – Mike Jewett

Mike Jewett is the editor and publisher of Boston Poetry Magazine (http://bostonpoetry.wordpress.com). He has been published most recently in Orion Magazine, Nostrovia! Poetry, and The Bitchin' Kitsch. His poetry has been compared to, among others, Van Gogh and Dylan Thomas. By day, he is a web developer. He has an amazing wife and a truly awesome son.

Krakatoa, 1883

You are a soft bed of dirt.
I am water, telling you I'll hold you
but leaving and taking pieces with me.
We live in 1883, and you have cultivated
a mountain that you keep your thoughts inside.

One A.M., Perth falls quiet;
your Mountain erupts.
Two A.M., I black out and come to;
what we've said has put holes in the wall.
Three A.M., my waves awake.
Like the body they spawn from,
they are uncontrolled.
I am sorry.
Four A.M., your mountain is gone;
my sea is ash-covered.

You lay still, the land that you fostered looking weak.

I no longer crash against you, I ebb and I flow.
Each rise and fall of tide is a gentle kiss.
That night I took the ash you poured across my body.
I let it soak and listened to the mountain's words.

Our island is smaller; instead of taking more away,
I will bring more to you.
And we will be an island again, your soft bed of dirt
growing slowly outwards.
I am four seas that girth you.

– Daniel Walden

Daniel Walden is a full-time college student from Jacksonville, Florida. He writes poetry, bizarre short stories and spends his free time exploring the riverside area around his home with his girlfriend and his cat.

I have met you

I have met you in photographs
and photo-memories.
Sometimes, I remember
places I have never been at all.

But there are violet skies,
a wooden bench under my hands,
hot bread and butter, melting onto plates
and the warmth of you beside me.

I know you
through other people's stories.
A million different gospels and recollections
and mixed-up names so that,
a child detective,
I have pieced together an amazing magazine cut-out
with a synthetic nose and eyes and voice
and teeth,
a model of you,
as if I might even have known you
before we walked different planes.

I have loved you.

Her rabbit is under my bed,
green curtain dress, soft face all bare
and if I touch it,
the threads will fall apart
like white worms under my fingertips,
and all the stitches will unravel
and the stuffing will leak from its body
so I don't touch it,
and it is like her
and I must leave it alone.

– Sophie Howard

Sophie Howard studied English Literature and Creative Writing at Aberystwyth University. She is currently living in the North-East of England with a tomato plant and a sunflower.

Precision Forever Eludes Us

When I swerve to pounce
I know! I am sure! I trap it with a single clasp!
Harvest-full my hands are, with precious, rarest cargo.

Yet when I open them, they dangle
bereft and bare.

When I nail it on the board for spread-eagled scrutiny,
its beating heart flutters elsewhere.
Missing the target, pinpricks will render
Superficial shrills into confetti thrills.
No capture, falling,

        F

             all

                      ing

Quick shake-off -
nothing but dust -
back in ring to entice and encircle
voluptuous forevers and nevers,
untamed, unbowed, unrepentant.

I always fail.
Is there a point in trying?

Defeat feels anything but...
Next time -
always next time -
the vision will be luminous.
Sounds will surge forth, perfectly aligned.
Until then...

Here's to the missing.

– Marina Sofia

Marina Sofia is a global nomad, currently living near Geneva, Switzerland. She has recently found her way back to poetry and published in Offshoots, Respiro, When Women Waken and an anthology of Western haiku. She is also part of the editorial team of the online dVerse Poets Pub.

Waiting at Stop 37

Waiting in gusty shades of grey
squinting as the sharp tram screeches
the brown skeletons line the street
with emerald leaves falling like rain
bursting with pink flower petals.
They are not originally from here
elms and oaks from northern kinsfolk
weather the storms with native gums.
Some will breathe the howls of nature
some will tremor under her roars
some will resign beneath the ground.
Inside, lines will tell their story
Outside, they make their community.

– Charlie Alford

Charlie Alford is a small town English girl living in metropolitan Melbourne, a city at the bottom of the world. When she's not confined to her day job she's out in the world observing and creating. She loves to write poetry, bake cupcakes and create calligraphy and iPhotography.

Arnold Schwarzenegger in New York, 1968

And he thought he was big.

He was always seen in his buttoned-up hometown –
towering like a mythical hillock over
market crowds,
shouldering shelves of modest jams
out of place in simple shops,
or knocking hooked sides of beef like church bells in
the set butcher's.

For his big trip to New York
Arnold arrived swaddled in a clotted cardigan of
Austrian wool.
His perfection of hair was embarrassed by its
traditionalism.
The levitating camera, a chunk of metal, looked
worried in his Herculean fingers.
But despite his obvious preparedness, his car-wide
shoulders, his tree trunk neck,
his negroid nose and his girder-like legs,
Arnold's little face was rapt with the everywhere-ness
of the city
and his own dwarfing.

Looking innocent, on the spot, his sunned features
wondered at the upward audacity
of skyscrapers.
Arnold felt a kinship with them, like that which a
young boy has with older, exotic cousins.
For hours he could have remained dreaming into
minute windows
overcome by New York's bigness
but after such a successful regression
the project of his remodelling had to be accelerated.

– James Nixon

James Nixon is a writer, poet and editor from London. He is studying
Creative Writing at postgraduate level at Royal Holloway, University
of London. His work has been published variously, and he is the editor
of the poetry platform Fry Your Friends. You can follow him on
Twitter (@j_a_nixon) or visit fryyourfriends.wordpress.com.

Lines on my younger paranoia

I wish you'd stop staring,
your gaze is burning the
rope that elevates my cool;
tethers melt my lifeline,
remind me of just how cruel
this world I live in can be.

While my desires of a Palomino
and a six foot, jet black, kick ass
warrior princess perform in my
cerebral theatre,
a simmering saucer of fury
Ii emulating: crimson like the shade

of my chubby cheeks, contrasts
with a tone of lonesome weeks.
Can you see my reaper too?
the hooded phantom that
visits me at night, gets a
kick from delivering me fright.

Or the time I sobbed my eyes raw
because of the horned monster who
lived under my floor;
you can see mine, but you
have a filter, or a shield:
one not likely to ever yield.

'How is it fair?' I ask the bearded
man upstairs. You are meant to love
me, you are the deity that cares!
What shall I do now, except
attempt the impossible
and make my thoughts invisible?

– Thomas Dockerill

Thomas Dockerill is a 20 year old English Literature student from West
Yorkshire, studying at Aberystwyth University. He enjoys writing and
performing poetry, and occasionally stand up comedy. A true
romantic, he's always seeking love; but the only birds that seem
interested are the flappy ones chasing him down the promenade.

Sleepy Sandcastles

Speckled, freckled
Cheeks a fluster
Digging, patting
Sandcastles glister
Roaring, soaring
Kites roam blue
Frothy, toffee
Cappuccino waves
Bring dancing white horses
To wriggling free toes
Hiding, sliding
On the hilly high
Dunes
Ducking, looking
Glimpsing and waiting,
For the seeker to peek
As you saunter downhill
And rush through the bush
But now here it is,
Our time is to stop,
Because here the day
Starts a beautiful end,
Cuddling up
Ready to rest,

Just enough time
To sit and mellow
Now the sky darkens
And turns less yellow
In the car
Windows ajar
Sleepy sighs
Speckled, freckled
Cheeks a fluster.

– Kirsty Higginson

Kirsty Higginson is a poet, writer, and freelance journalist. She resides amongst the luxurious, cobbled streets of Lancashire. In her spare time, she dreams of conquering the world with Doctor Who and runs the Left in Preston arts project. You can find a collection of her work at https://talltalesoffiction.wordpress.com.

War's Song

The wait is a pale stretch of quivering lip
shrouded by echoing steal, bent like beamed bone.
You rattled away like gun fire, as the black cable coiled
around the corner
and puffed a fug with a hiss,
whilst I waved a white flag kiss to your sliver of back
and hummed Vera Lynn to calm the wobbling chords.
My soldier boy, drumming on pistons, away to war.

The days without you curled into weeks and blackened
in the blitz.
I swallowed your words from letters read in blackout
light;
they were as precious as a prayer.
I wore them like armour, best, when the bombs were
falling
bursting through people's front doors with a Luftwaffe
kick,
and I helped mothers to rebirth their children, once
more, from ruins -
all marble still.
I snagged splinters of you in their endless rows.

THE WAIT

In a dream, last week, you were wet through,
and your kiss tasted like salt rot,
your fingers felt like wood knots.
I woke to the ghostly tune of your herringbone ribs
haunting under my palms.

Yesterday, two of Tommy's boys, with winter eyes,
handed me a telegram punctuated by a boot heel click.
I choked and hacked on their barbs.
You'd been killed with a cordite kiss,
left like a shell on the beach
you would be worn down to the consistency of sand.

With a swallow's knowledge I returned to our farewell;
a war widow, a martyr to the Nazi march.
The waiting, finally, ended like a sigh
and died with a last breath.

– Victoria David

Victoria David is an English Literature and Creative Writing graduate of Aberystwyth University. Victoria is twenty-one and this is her second poem to be published as part of an anthology. The first was 'Numinous', published in *Make Time for Aberystwyth* in 2014.

Treading Water

The hat of the old church sits above the water.
As children my brother and I took turns diving
down to the old town beneath the dam water.
Pulling ourselves along the steeple, to the rooftop
spine and staring blind into the stained windows
pulling ourselves under the broken rafters with the
fish.

We dreamt of treasure, of fishing pocket watches
out of old jackets found in houses, before burning
bodies forced us panicked for air to the surface.
Our old neighbour remembers nothing better
than crow stew that year. He tells us people
were crazed. Pets vanished. Sometimes children.

When we break the still, glassy water, it sprays
around us and we are baby birds fluttering
in puddles. The old, gone people, quiet beneath us.
Neither of us manage to touch the bottom,
find roads or the roots of streetlights.
Our game ends, floating on the dam surface

breathless and exhausted. Our limbs shake,
half drowning on the swim to shore, my brother,
Tommy, red, hearty half pulling me on,
before we tread water. We are peaceful.
Before suddenly he is snatched ankle first
                          and dragged beneath us.

– Leonie J Campbell

Leonie J Campbell, originally from the West Midlands, is 24 years old and currently based in Aberystwyth. Awaiting the start of an MA in Creative Writing, her interests include, but are not limited to, poetry, drinking copious amounts of tea, collecting books and playing the accordion.

Hair Lines

Goose bumps are leaving trails
on my skin
like routes for the tiny deer
which I suppose must live in your fingertips.

– Rhiannon Caitlin Morgan

Rhiannon Caitlin Morgan is a part time ice cream scooper and part time outdoor explorer with a fondness for bears and other hairy mammals. Her hamster, Lord Hal, enjoys exploring her desk space and distracting her from the writing she should be doing. You can find more of her work at Chicago-roses.tumblr.com.

Since you asked...

I'm not too good at the moment
I've a rather troubling cough
and my insides feel like they're burning
and my toenails need cutting off.

I've a touch of fungal infection
in a private place 'down below'
and I'd tell you how I caught it
but you really don't want to know.

I've got galloping alopecia
and a terrible crick in my neck
my shoulders and hips are giving me jip
all in all I'm a bit of a wreck.

My head is pounding from migraine
I've a blister from my shoe
But enough about me,
how's the cancer ward
and how are they treating you?

– Michele Brenton

Michele Brenton was born exactly 47 years after Dylan Thomas in Swansea. As banana_the_poet she was voted most popular human poet in the Twitter Shorty Awards 2011. She is delighted, surprised and honoured each time her work is included in a publication. It happened first in 2001.

Hard Copy

A promenade, the visible stretch
of shop fronts not yet shuttered up
for good. It must be one summer;
the street swells with afternoon crowds
and the sun slants into our eyes, so mine
are narrowed, when,
from behind the camera,
a call insists on smiles.

In the second we're committed
to the reel's impression, I manage it;
my hand has slipped routinely
into yours, its firmness, both of us younger
than we'd ever be again. Your patterned skirt
dazzles, as if super-imposed over
the grainy back-drop, setting the page
suddenly out of focus.

– Daniel Williams

Daniel Williams is a 22 year old poet, writer and photographer based in Aberystwyth. He graduated from Aberystwyth University in 2014 with a degree in English Literature and Creative Writing. His work has appeared in publications including The Cadaverine, Ink Sweat and Tears and Cheval 7. He is the editor of Long Exposure Magazine, which collects poetry and photography from around the world.

'Thinking through the skin'-
Natasha Mayo

Cardigan baptized me into town
when I first washed from
the taps of SA43 1QA

a soft type of water
flat fewer chemicals
reacted with my foreign composition.

The smoothness of my forearm
swelled uneven hills of rash-pimpled
pores protruding portraying

place, in dermatological form
of Cardigan's landscape
to cleanse my system of London,

to stress prick push place out
like sweat through the skin's plugholes,
as if in cultural exorcism.

– Keely Celia Laufer

Keely Celia Laufer is studying for a BA in English Literature and
Creative Writing at Aberystwyth University. She has had two poems

published in anthologies prior to 'Thinking through the skin'. Keely's current research interest centres on sites of the body as places to explore concepts of identity.

Mrs Smithfield

Mrs Smithfield writes an ode,
      and like a spy
      quietly slips
the blue lined pages
to me.
        Her soft brown cardigan
          – mohair –
        sheds tiny pearlescent stud buttons.
We live in canvas bells for five days
of sweaty, clammy, shelter,
          hot in fields of hay,
          as a great war rages.
Anne and I become snake
          and snake charmer
around a smoky campfire.
The menfolk are on the front
          – some of our dads are there –
they kill.
My dad's a Local Defence Volunteer. He has a gun.
        We have a singsong. *Pack Up Your*
        Troubles for wide-eyed mothers,
      nurses, head-scarfed land girls,
and munitions factory workers, yellow-faced canary
girls,

who feast on fat pork spitting

splitting sausages that stay

on the tongue with charred onion breath, for hours.

We wonder what it's like

on the bloody muddy Western front.

If You Were The Only Girl In The World…

The mothers' eyes shine.

The big blue-garbed girl guides,

tease us because we're brown

– no pearl buttons –

Me, arms akimbo, in a khaki sleeping bag;

writhing, serpentine,

up and down,

side to side,

while Anne tootles, fluting on her recorder,

face dark with gravy browning.

In the trenches, guns shatter eardrums, pop eyeballs,

make mush of bones.

The big girls give out smelly rubber gas masks

– it's hard to breathe –

they send messages using small flags;

wrinkle soapy fingers in hospitals, lather and

launder dressings,

roll bandages, prep stretchers for bleeding bodies.

We collect warm hens' eggs, harvest cabbages and

keep our chins up,

knit socks and scarves for the Tommies,
>   and hope our mums don't get a telegram.
And later, as we lend a hand and do our best and serve
our King,
Mrs Smithfield
>   quietly slips
the blue lined pages
>   with a faint crackle
>   and an apologetic air,
to me.

– Polly Robinson

Polly Robinson is a member of Worcester Writers' Circle and part of the Worcestershire Literary Festival team. She performs her poetry at various venues including The Poetry Place in Covent Garden. Her writing has been published in anthologies and she released *Girl's Got Rhythm* in 2012 and *Chatterton* in 2014.

Circle Dance

Tell me why we dance the round
fingertips touching
feet on the ground.
This sweet wine tastes
of bitter allows,
mother's ruin,
sloes and arrows.
We spin around
and you leave me reeling,
the Judas kiss
was still deceiving.
I pledged to you
a barbed ring oath,
life shot me down
and stole your troth.

– Alexandra Carr-Malcolm

Alexandra Carr-Malcolm, a British Sign Language Interpreter, lives in Yorkshire. Featured in five collaborative anthologies, her first collection *Tipping Sheep (the right way)* was released in 2013. She is currently working on her second collection. Her poetry focuses on the human predicament.

5 am

It's strange how when I hold a pen
it comes alive at 5am.
It dances on the page, just then,
with unexpected grace.
No words came forth during the night;
no masterpiece that I could write.
But close to dawn, in the half-light
my words assume their place.
No cause for pressure or for force,
the writer's block shows full remorse.
Musings to words, they run their course
paper and ink embrace.
Perhaps the stillness of the air,
the tranquillity, sparks the flare
of the inspiration so rare
it seldom helps to chase.
At 5am, the world's asleep.
The silence settles in so deep
together with my thoughts, to keep
a comfortable pace.
At this small hour, there's nothing to
claim my attention like you do -
though merely this brief thought of you
gives my heart leave to race.

And all at once I understand:
I cannot write if I have planned
to keep vacant my writing hand
reasoning "just in case";
in case your own demands my touch
though you've not asked outright, as such.
My mind's eye isn't fit for much
when blinded by your face.
As 5am slips off the clock
I realise you're my mental block.
Perhaps for now I'll turn the lock -
see if I can replace
your presence in the thoughts I think
with words that teeter on the brink
of newfound treasures, made of ink.
Wonders could fill your space.

– Hannah Price

Hannah Price is a shop assistant by day and an aspiring writer by night. She spends a lot of time in her very purple flat, singing along to loud music and scribbling her thoughts in one of the hundreds of pretty notebooks which she has an addiction to buying.

A slightly fictional thing that happened

You are cold and it is spring
lemonade hisses as it meets the glass
& I've never felt flatter -
I mean I would rather crawl
heavily along ugly broken mirrors
uglier than air, uglier than kisses
raindrops hate reflections chewed apples fat divorcees
halves of a whole
I would rather burn away my skin
burn away my veins the flimsy subtext
that they are
than continue to carry you around with me

I hand you your glass, a sober old highball
you drink it in
leaving your imprint at its edge
and I can't help but find it funny
knowing how it feels. But I don't laugh.
you pull a face and your nose wrinkles
it looks like a tiny old lady living
under your eyes. (don't worry this won't be
another poem describing eyes)
it couldn't be even if I wanted it to,
it's finished now

– Sean Macro

Sean Macro is a writer and poetry editor at Dagda Publishing. His work has appeared in The Flaneur, Dead Beats Literary Blog, Mad Swirl and others in print and online. His debut pamphlet, *Happy Hour at the Misery Bar*, was released in 2013.

The Lost Hive

I suffered your desire
A feeling that was most dire
Lord have mercy
Deliver me from this little tantrum

You kept gazing at the stars
and ignored what I offered
You said I brought home everything
but what you wanted
Maybe you never knew
what that was

I'm taking the train home
while you keep pounding
A million doves flew
after our story ended
It wasn't on a cold Sunday
but on a warm Thursday

Those cherry tulips that grew
Why did you stomp on them?
We both knew about the fire that burnt
I didn't suspect my role as a stopgap
Whir yourself around once more
Maybe the fire will be put out

Your reflection on the television has faded
Well, I guess that's entertainment
You were deaf to all my pleas
Was it the wasps in your ears?
See me chew through these killer bees
More dignified than being on my knees

We knew what would put us back together right
All the paintings skewed slight to the right
wore our coat of arms on our hearts
and that combative monster that saw us by the river
still stands upright, his memory remembers most
while all we felt has turned to dust.

– Samuel Valdés López

Sam Valdes Lopez enjoys the many pleasures of multisyllabic words
that he can't rightly pronounce but enjoys writing.

King Microwave

Oh microwave upon the floor
Who guards the sink-side cupboard door,
Why do you sit so neat and proud
Within your torn-up-package shroud?

What heart have you to bear such zeal
For such a piece of moulded steel;
What triumphs do you long to suit
To pride amongst your cardboard loot?

Oh microwave, who put you there?
Who gave you such a box to wear?
You are so small and upside down,
But do you dream a golden crown?

Do you think of some great throne,
Of places you could call your own?
Do you dream of kingdoms high,
And one true name that rules the sky?

'Oh Microwave!' you wish they'd cheer,
With beaming grin from ear to ear,
And with a better voice than ours
You'd love and hate with all your powers:

THE WAIT

Not sixty watts, but sixty gems;
With rubies scattered at your hems,
Your gown of silver, not of card,
And actions named by bard and bard!

Oh Microwave, how well I see,
You're just a dreaming whim like me;
So keep your kingdom, dream some more,
You ruler of the kitchen floor.

– Mike Steel

Mike - he was a simple lad,
    His poetry was rather bad,
    Once he saw a microwave
    And that was it from birth to grave.
    One thing in life he did not do
    Was finish off this

Portrait When It's Gloomy

My girl is but a sea-side hotel,
I'm barely a pinball machine,
I keep firing up and falling in between the kickers,

I'm barely a pool table
And the corner can't get clogged,
And on the emerald felt, my girl is feeling left out,

I chased her into the gardens,
I cried into her Koi pond,
I molested Venus on crunchy gravel,
It broke rhythm over my song,

I painted all day 'til my hands were blue,
I called to say 'sorry' but couldn't get through,
I'm bouncing off obstacles,
I'm sinking on a green lake,
My girl is but a sea-side hotel,
And on the beach I'm a wave yet to break

– James Traylen

James Traylen lives in the South of England with his Ma and Pa and his two older brothers. He is eighteen, and has never had to personally experience the effects of cancer. He hopes he never will. He likes pizza and the Beach Boys.

Old Boots

Old boots
Proud, supple
Tough comfort
Snug, worn
Waiting to leave again

Bends, edges
Marked forever
Evergreen tinges
Memory ties
In the right places
Laces knot
On end, anew

Old lace for new lanes
Reboot

– Adura Ojo

Adura Ojo is a blogger, writer and a mother of two. She lives in the UK. Her poems have been published in Poetic Pinup Revue, Sentinel Nigeria, and on websites. Her debut poetry collection, *Life is a Woman Breaking Eggs* is to be published September 2014. You can read more of her work at http://adura-ojo.blogspot.com, or follow her on Twitter (@AduraOjo).

Grand-dad's Eightieth

He's reading his cards;
a hand takes them away as he finishes,
while another one replaces them.
I don't know much about turning eighty,
but people keep loading significance
on to the passing of each decade, as if to say:
'That's it; this is the zenith!

Congratulations.
Enjoy your twilight years;
read, play golf, go on cruises;
we'll take care of things now.'

Mum reads the cards aloud
as she takes them away from him,
collects the wrapping that he discards,
and when we get up to leave,
checks that he hasn't forgotten his wallet.

We make a rare visit to an expensive restaurant.
Grand-dad orders lobster,
and it arrives with its pink shell unbroken,
complemented by a brace of green vegetables,
steaming up a wonderful smell.

THE WAIT

He tucks his napkin into his collar,
and begins:

His knife does not quiver
as he beheads the crustacean with one stab
to the back of the neck, and the fork is steady
in his grip, keeping the creature from scuttling
off the china; he meticulously disembowels it,
and rolls the soft meat around his tongue.
The claws now; mum offers to help with the break
but he swipes the tool with a polite 'no thank you'
and cracks the shell, baring his teeth and enjoying
himself.
Flecks of shell and meat are sprayed over his napkin;
he cracks a joke, and we all laugh with him.

He's taking me to an air show next weekend.
I'll look forward to seeing him all week, and you
know –
that won't rely on the past eighty years
of his life at all.

– Vish Amarasinghe

Vish Amarasinghe is a recent graduate of Aberystwyth University. His
interest in poetry grew through writing songs, and the setting of words
to music. He is 21 years old.

The gift of touch

Your touch returns
slowly
the last thing to recover
from the years of neglect

Feeling it now startles me
like an electric shock
left for a moment
unable to breathe

I am thankful
to rediscover a lost sense
and for skin
to absorb you into my heart

Longing for you
I imagine you forever
stuck to me like honey
a gift from the bees
to hold us to each other

– Daniel von der Embse

Daniel von der Embse began writing poetry after a 37-year career as a
writer for advertising agencies in New York, Chicago, Los Angeles,

Seattle, San Francisco, and Salt Lake City. His poems appear in The Missing Slate, The Laughing Dog, Decanto, Woven Tale Press, Aberration Labyrinth, Poetry Pacific, and Poetry Quarterly.

In Memoriam

"J. Cecil Jones, memorial specialists
– for excellence, why pay more?"
I wonder, what's a little death
between friends with benefits?

If not for excellence, then why pay more?
Blank gravestones fill the shop front,
and a corpse has no kind of value left
– it needs little more than a trap door.

A blank gravestone from the shop front
sisters blank sheets and an empty bed,
where la petite mort spent a last breath.
Though, it sounded like more of a grunt.

Twisted stained sheets make a busy bed.
"J. Cecil Jones, memorial specialists;
where la petite mort rings out with a grunt
– for excellence, I'd pay more."

– Morgan Roberts

Morgan Roberts was
Once upon a time
Really small and,
Granted, he's not
Amazingly tall
Now but he is larger.

January Night

I remember the very first gift you gave
to me; not merely your untamed beauty
but love-black words, bound; spine unstitched, I save
that memory; the dissonance behind me,
unclutterable trains unhinged; a sad, black tinge
in my eyes, I read, bent like a horizon
that swallows the sea. The moon was orange
above me, in my heart, two hearts you had undone
like silver strings of stars, or ribbons, red;
you tugged. You tugged at the threads of my dreams
but left them unbroken, fragile, half-fed.

– Ianto Jones

Ianto Jones is a twenty-year-old poet and songwriter from Cardiff, in
his spare time he studies English and Creative Writing at Aberystwyth
University. He revels in reading Jack Kerouac novels and listening to
Elliott Smith. He also has a penchant for World Cinema, River Phoenix
and red wine.

Early

I want to wake up on Saturday morning
with sunshine warming the back of the house.
It's early because I slept well
not because I didn't sleep.
I want to go downstairs,
watch cartoons, and not be afraid
to eat toast.
Uncle Bob and Martyn Goodacre
listen to Nevermind, oblivious
- he really does have a gun.
The worst pain is a scraped knee
and it's the kind of pain
I can tell Mum and Dad.

If you could go back,
would you?
Be careful what you wish for.
It isn't just life that's changed
- it's us, too.

– Tricia Clare Onions

Tricia Clare Onions was born in Worcestershire. When she's not writing, she also enjoys playing guitar and making the perfect cup of coffee. She studied English and Creative Writing at Aberystwyth University and is currently taking the subject at postgraduate level in Birmingham.

Too Scared To Wake

I dream of hills and mountains high,
Of crisp green grass and deep blue sky,
The call of birds 'til dusk, from dawn,
As flowers spread across the lawn.
The sun is high, both warm and bright,
The moon; a silver torch at night.
And there, atop the mountains tall,
A young girl stands, prepared to fall.

Her hands are damaged, dripping blood,
Her eyes red from the salty flood.
And there she stays, from dawn 'til dusk,
Fading to a shadowy husk.
She does not move, but for her hair
Which rides the wind; a stream of fair.
Her skin is pale, her features small,
And yet through this she does not fall.

But when I wake, her legs will give,
And then no more her soul shall live.

– Sarah Sommerville

Morning

The dawn was silent; the forest was cold.
A red deer buck strode out from the trees,
his strong form stood watching, proud and bold.

The leaves in the trees glowed red and gold
as autumnal sun lit the wood with ease.
The dawn was silent; the forest was cold.

The leaf litter was strewn, uncontrolled,
blown by a faint and calming breeze.
His strong form stood watching, proud and bold.

The hunter watched, knew what would unfold.
He crouched down on his hands and knees.
The dawn was silent; the forest was cold.

The rifle rested firmly in his hold.
He pulled the trigger down with a squeeze.
The dawn was silent; the forest was cold.
His strong form stood watching, proud and bold.

– Alex Harden

Alex Harden is a writer and poet living in the UK, he's a self-confessed
eco-poet and lover of nature, most of what he writes winds up having

something to do with it anyway. He runs a blog called WordofAlexicon on Wordpress, which is his own space for his writing, photography and reviews.

Dog Years

The dandy crow with treacle back arches
Laughs at the dog that twitches in darkness
In every light there is a shadow
Graphite, charcoaled molecules
They gain form to separate us
To choreograph a tease
A reminder of the heart that hangs low at the gallows.

I lied about my age. Friend.
For I am old.
Below this ivory skin, glow on lip,
I've lived ten thousand times the average girl.
These dog years.

– Heather E Andrews

Heather Andrews hails from the moors of Ayrshire, where she likes to write at night when bodies are asleep and dreams are awake. She has been published in a number of poetry anthologies and, most recently, Octavius magazine. She is currently working on her debut novel.

Bedroom

I used to sleep like this before
under gold curtains,
second-hand, and each night
above glass I counted
stars three for Orion six
for the Plough and nine
for wishes that never did come true

– Rebecca McCormick

Rebecca McCormick is a bookkeeper by day and an artist by night. She is currently studying for her MA in Writing at Sheffield Hallam University, with a particular interest in Writing for Children. She always wears dresses and owns far too much nail polish.

the promenade

a springgrey backdrop
the air thick with the suggestion of rain and the
battered remnants of a wave against the barrier
catches an eyelash and triggers the memory of
tears burning and the last time your fingers
left my hand with a worried smile
an atmosphere of gulls and pigeons bloody rats
with wings encases me in the image of you
sitting there alone with an ice cream and a mood
of bittersweet thoughts crossing your eyes
telling me you're fine when i knew you were
missing a part of your reason for living
the sound of seashells drowning out the low
humming nonsense of those around me when
all i can picture is your unhappiness and what
an untimely end they say and it's true and now
i'm the one sitting here alone facing a vast space
of ruthlessness as the waves are unforgiving to
all with no special selection i suppose that's
life and this is it and i have to carry on despite
the you-shaped void that appears to be hurting
my ability to understand that things just happen
and there is no going back even if at the end of it
all we never had a chance to say goodbye and the

grey sky grey sea jolts me from my black and white
perception of the way things work and now i am
grey grey grey without you.

– Ffion Wyn Morris

Ffion Wyn Morris is a poet who originally hails from a small town in
the mountains of North Wales. She uses her own experiences to craft
spoken word pieces that often meander between the Welsh and English
languages. Now living and working full-time in Cardiff, she spends her
evenings and weekends planning an escape route.

To Remember

The eyes never seem to forget, even if
the limbs do, and the frailty seems unsupported,
and is allowed free reign over arms and joints.

The radio, now taken apart for the third time,
with hands that were always so precise, like
a kestrel's swoop, like a watchmaker's eye.

That slight glitch of recognition rarely makes
up for that lost movement, that leaves that
footprint, which then dissolves in the slightest
breeze.

– Jonathan Butcher

Jonathan Butcher is a poet based in Sheffield. He has had poetry appear
in various print and online publications, both in the UK and US. His
second chapbook, *Broken Slates*, was published by Flutter Press.

Snow

The heights of air became a place of flitting hurry,
The fluttering silence was full of memory.
Frozen flecks floated in the tall grey whiteness,
A dusky gloom feathered with brightness.
And within this infinite carousel the maid crying bitterly,
Fell into the downy arms of snow and sought kindness.

– Hannah Davies

Hannah Davies grew up mostly in Pembrokeshire, got her English
degree in London, and is now a Library Assistant. She lives in Cardiff
with her husband Alec, in an old terraced house with a sunny garden.
She is touched by the support of friends and family for her literary
adventures.

The Beauty of the Beast

She came to me in winter -
cloaked in blizzards -
shards of ice, fine
as splintered glass.
Beauty was a pale myth,
a frozen carcass
beneath the snow.
Ripe buds struggled
to the surface
and suffocated at my touch.

Time's fingers peeled
a palace's gilt walls
and turned the halls to ash.
Cracked tea sets,
cold candlesticks
locked behind glass,
choked in dust.
Gone were the days they'd dance,
light-footed between the pillars of dawn
that burned through the halls.

Within these darkened passages
a bell jar held my soul in bloom

flushing crimson
through the lasting night.
With a calculated motion
it shed its petals, one by one,
with the marching of the years.
And those petals grew ever sparse.

It was the solstice of our hearts,
but she ran her fingers through my fur,
dull from those sun-starved years,
and called it Beauty.
A word as rare as the two of us.
A Beauty and a Beast.

She brought with her the summer
short-lived, as sweet things are.
We lay entwined,
bare skin on matted fur,
and desperate pleas
escaped my jaws.
Love me. Save me.
But she would not.

And as the last petal shuddered
on its fragile stem
she let the gales sweep back

through the hollow halls.
I stretched my paws to draw her near.
She caught my claws.
Drew blood.
Fled.

I starved myself of my usual feasts
of carrion and smaller beasts
and hoped the skeleton of a man
would drop from my pelt
and she'd return
as love always does.

Love, if your honeyed words
were said with truer intent
than to please the ear
you would have stayed
to see this curse broken.
But it takes more than one short summer
for a Beast to shed his skin.
The love that's said to save a prince
is not a brief exchange
of tender words
nor a fleeting kiss.
It's as steadfast
as the palace stone.

Inked with time,
but enduring the ages
and the tempests they bring.

I know these tales as old as time
and believe them to be true,
but living among happy endings
I found my strength in solitude
so when beauty returns to these halls
it will find man and beast reconciled.
Clumps of fur will line the floor,
the heavy windows shattered
and my friends will dance again
in fields of light.
Love will see through a monster's shell
to the human heart beneath.

– Poppy Tester

Poppy Tester is inspired by fairy tales, Arthurian legend and just old things in general. She's not ashamed to say that Disney's *Beauty and the Beast* is the best film she's ever seen. She watched it while writing this poem. In fact, she's probably watching it as you read this.

Antimatter

It's a heavy weight to carry
the antimatter in the spaces
where you were

but I've borne it for years
carried it on my back
like a held breath
in my lungs and
all across my chest.

you are in all my atoms
you are nowhere else
and the world is heavier for it

(sometimes I think that must be why
the days go slower sometimes)

sometimes I think the world spins on its axis
for want of you
and sometimes I think
it never even
moves
at all.

THE WAIT

It is all a youless Ulysses
a stream of consciousness and
spiderweb thoughts.
It is all the places you are not

and I carry the weight
and I will carry the weight
and there is no pastpresentfuture
only nowthen
and always
alwaysalwaysalways where are you
and willyoucomenowplease
it's dark and we're
somewhere wrong.

There's no getting over it
no *the first year is the hardest, you know*
or *it hurts at first, but -*

there's only one year
then two years
then three years
then four

and it is all the same
and there is nothing else to it
it is such a heavy weight.

– Anwen Hayward

Anwen Hayward is a mass of chemical and organic matter made from the remnants of supernovas and old atoms. Her hobbies include respiration, frustration and ennui. She is a graduate of English and Creative Writing from Aberystwyth University, where the fates aligned and permitted her a First in her dissertation.

Seven Foot Stinger

I'm your friendly seven-foot super-Sized Stinging
Nettle
Into MY lair you stray
Should you display enough mettle
I work 24 hours, in a 7 day week
The misery for every garden I seek.
Leaves like the size of the back of an iron
Your skin scrapes with mine, and you'll roar like a lion
You'll find no other weed in as fine a fettle
As your friendly Seven-Foot Super Sized Stinging
Nettle
A deadly threat to any would-be Hansel and Gretel
Who'd go jigging around the wrong gingerbread house
I grow around inside it, quiet as a mouse
Like the mugger that awaits you
Down each public path
I'll hang through and prang you
Ain't my life a laugh?
As joggers so stupid as not to wear sleeves
Suffer the ammo of my lethal green leaves
You'll need to grow armour of galvanised metal
To survive the might of Seven-Foot Super-Sized
Stinging Nettle
I grow in graveyards and garages

Abandoned in years
Seeking revenge on my friends that ended as beer
I'd shoot through your flowers with my savage green
gloat
Like the bit on *Jaws 2* when he comes up through the
boat
You'll die of one bite from the brutal-toothed petals
Of me, the Seven Foot Super-Sized Stinging Nettle
My pain travels fast as Sebastian Vettel
Drive through all daisies that dare stand in my way
You daffodils, petunias and pansies will pay
Even the prickliest of brambles stand no ice cream on
Hell's chance
Of shielding you from my sharp-like-razor's advance
So set down your spade, your fork and your rake
While I still haven't sensed you, there's still a chance to
make break
'Cos you'd rather the scold of a piping hot kettle
Than a encounter with the Seven-Foot Super Sized
Stinging Nettle

– Dave Attrill

Dave Attrill is a poet/novelist from Sheffield. He has released two books
- a novel called *Playground* and a poetry collection called *Battenberg
and Brain Damage*. He has been published in several WEA anthologies,
and performs frequently at open mic literature events across Yorkshire
and Chesterfield.

Exponential

You're far from gone,
You helped me reach my potential,
And I'll do the same for someone else
Because you're exponential.

– Joseph Purcell McAlister

Joseph Pursell McAlister resides in Orangevale (Sacramento County), California with his wife, Stacie, and son, Jack. He works as a high school special education teacher at Casa Roble High School. The form of poetry he enjoys the most is micropoetry (poems written with 140 characters or less).

3 a.m.

We dozed off holding hands but I woke up
with a start. Maybe you'd pulled your hand away
or perhaps I'd relaxed my grip but I'd felt you
slipping through my fingers.

I grabbed your hand so tight you asked,

'Are you OK?'

And I heard myself reply,

'I just woke up with a start…'

But I'd felt you slipping through my fingers.

You put your arms around me
and we cuddled up real tight as
silent tears rolled down my cheeks.
I don't know if you'd noticed;
you were wearing thick pyjamas
but you held on really tight.

My turn to ask,

'Are you OK?

'I'm OK,' you said, with a catch voice.

We were not being honest and
we were both in need of sleep.
And it didn't seem like the right time
to talk about the possibility
of goodbye.

– Karen Harvey

Karen Harvey is a poet and artist who lives by the sea. Keeping a
journal throughout the journey as she accompanied her husband
through tests, diagnoses and treatment of early prostate cancer helped
her deal with the emotional impact of the situation. Her husband is
now all clear.

The Dinner Table

I can hear my parents arguing from the lawn.
Fighting fork with fork,
they are swordsmen,
weighing the credits of ketchup against brown
as if life and death depends on it.

Click. The door sways apart like parting hands,
Ivory cogs gristle, turn and
creak.

The smell of thyme looks at me with fragrant eyes
like candles. I am the firefly
floating in
like they do in those cartoons;
six plates carted off to the table.

What's cooking?
No idea;
looks kind of green, I say;
family glares shoot me down.

Food glides in on a bed of white mist
like steamboats
while rowdy voices barter with space,

the best plates,
a place in time people called 'house'
but to us, it is home.

Hungry for drama
we sample nostalgic tales
over mahogany.
That scent never changes.

We say Grace,
thanking whatever God might or might not exist
for the brilliance of taking tins of beans
and adding sausages in,
lathering it on aromatic toast masterpieces.

We consume.
We share.
We digest.
We digress.

– Adam Morris

Adam Morris is a private tutor, working in places from Sheffield to Spain, feeding his passion to travel. His poem, however, is about the familiarity and often comic community of home life with his family. Admittedly he does miss them... sometimes.

Why I Love Physiology

I study the organic mechanics of every human on the planet. From cognitive psychology and clinical neurology to an astonishing understanding of human immunology. It's amazing to study aging, the science of dating and the neurons of tasting.

Presumably, my only chance to put a dead body under scrutiny and observe its ingenuity, I find the human construction through professor instruction and scientific deduction, though it is often incomprehensible, it is hands down incredible.

But hands up if you've heard that you come to university just to 'find yourself'? Wouldn't it be fun to put that on the shelf and instead study, well, yourself?

– Rachel Shannon

Rachel Shannon, 21, is a Physiology student from London who studies at Bristol University. She has written for her university's online newspaper, for whatsonstage.com and has performed with Brushstrokes Theatre Company, as Puck in *A Midsummer Night's Dream*. Rachel loves making YouTube videos, blogging and writing spoken word poetry.

a little night music

late at night
the moon is high, yellow
and round as the big streetlamps
in the town across the bay

where a neon-flaring
curtain wall of waterfront bars and clubs
casts a net of noise over the water

stramash like a cliff-
full of kittiwakes, while
out here, where we are, the quiet water
whispers secrets against our hull

puttering port patrol boat
ticks to and fro like clockwork
bent on shattering the moon's golden sea-path

into an arpeggio of ripples

– Mandy Macdonald

Mandy Macdonald is an Australian writer living in Aberdeen. She has been writing poetry for ages, clandestinely, but is finally letting other people see it. She has had poems published in Haiku Scotland, Poetry Scotland, Pushing Out the Boat, The Stare's Nest, and Nutshells and Nuggets.

Christmas Eve 1962

Waiting until the very last, chances were we'd fail,
but youth being dauntless, my insistence prevailed.
We set off to buy a tree in the eleventh hour,
ornaments too; baubles, garland, tinsel,
and tit bits to sweeten the day for my dying
grandmother;
lemon nut cookies, pickled pigs' feet and kippers,
curled ribbon candy and thick, velvety eggnog with
rum.
I held tight to the traditions fast slipping away,
like my grandmother's days and my mother's
enthusiasm
and my brother and his wife's less frequent visits. I
knew
the truth about Christmas. Still I dreamed, fought the
changes
as I curled beneath my school desk for 'duck and cover'.
I'd waited, terrified, during the Bay of Pigs stand-off,
wanting some magic to chase nightmares away.

We laughed then, four voices raised in the night
through the streets I'd never seen so empty,
never walked this time of night on Christmas Eve,
always home with the magic I now saw, wouldn't come;

magic I'd need to create for myself. Then,
as our feet crunched the unblemished blanket,
the snow burst with purpose,
filling the streets faster than we walked.
In freeze time the silence fell,
deep and blue and surrounding,
light as the capture of a collective breath,
hung delicate as crystal, descending,
heavy with the weight of centuries.
The world stood still.

We all stood still.
Trapped in the frozen quiet
like flies in amber. My mother's lips,
my brother's eyes, my sister-in-law's cheeks
raised to the sky, as if awaiting a distant angelic
descent,
catching the snow as it fell through the street lamps'
glow.
Forever after, when I'd think of Christmas,
this moment would epitomise them all;
as in a captured breath, beauty to still the heart.
Who could ever have told us, how could we ever know
that the next year, the world would hold its breath,
for an era lost and a President's death,
for a new millennium, approaching too fast and,

that for me, this Christmas of childhood would be my last?

– Adele C Geraghty

Adele C Geraghty is the recipient of the US National Womens History Award for women's poetry and essay and author of the poetry collection *Skywriting in the Minor Key: women, words, wings*. She is also a member of New York's 'The Arts Soiree', a collective of artists of varying genre. She is Publisher of BTS Books and Poetry Editor of Gold Dust Magazine. She may be reached at BTSBooks2007@aol.com.

Tobacco grandfather

Never knowing you
is not the problem.
I smell you in the tobacco
brown photos.
I see you in the deep laughs
that spread to my father's eyes.
I hear you in his stories, his elbow-
rolled shirts.
The earth under your boots
turns from rich brown of the
allotment to the sands of
Africa to the grit of Dunkirk.
Rich browns of leather, wood
and dried, golden leaves. Curl up,
let the wind carry you.

– Kathryn Charlotte Hill

Kathryn Charlotte Hill studied English Literature at Aberystwyth University. She lives in Kent, working as an assistant editor and online editor for a magazine – all the while dreaming of running away to live in Paris.

Zombie nails

Prickling pressure
Sickening soreness
heralds the start

Tingling on plastic pads
Red, purple, creeping
sharply contrasts milky white tips

Pre-empting the finale,
zombie green and grey
Translucent fluid turns thick
Lifting, agonising, giving way
to the relentless pressure beneath

And yet the paradox
The stench and sight of decay
A visualisation
Of the destructive hope of salvation

– Julie May

Julie May lives with her husband and two children in West Wales. She loves animals and has a menagerie of horses, sheep, ducks and dogs. She is recovering from treatment for breast cancer. Her mum inspired her love of literature, reading many books to her and her sisters as children.

Sterile Soldiers

Huddled together,
sterile soldiers
waiting to be called.
Intermittent high-pitched screech
signals the beginning,
pacifies the drones.

White queen emerges
from the distant hollow
with a fixed waxy smile, promises hope;
salvation for the workers.

– Joy Sandifer

Joy Sandifer is a law lecturer living and working in West Wales. She is
passionate about education, good food and spending as much time as
possible enjoying the company of her family and friends.

THE WAIT

II

slip my features
into hers, long exposure
makes someone else
of us all
and I think
are we twinned by more than
thin hair like wires across pylons
Or the weft of my polyester top
umbilicling between us
do our thoughts touch too,
kiss and fizz
across the room, cubed,
or can we not tell until
a lens, click-
Click.

-Hannah Kelly

Hannah Kelly lives in Edinburgh, eats marshmallow fluff and writes.

Enough Stars

Did the sky cry again last night?
I whispered as you held me.
You never tend to dream
unless they're nightmares.
Either way you've always held me
to let me dream for both of us.

I don't see enough stars
unless I'm with you.
Even this heat isn't hot enough
without the beaches and picnics
I know you love,
that we've always loved.

We played pooh sticks together,
with your enthusiasm,
feeding the ducks and swans
and looking for Jemima.
Sometimes the fox too
if you're feeling silly enough.

THE WAIT

Since the storm cloud passed,
I'm glad for the rain.
They say it always rains here,
but that doesn't matter.
You always say it's good for the plants;
I believe you.

– Clover Reeds

Clover Reeds is an Oxford-based writer and artist.

Martian Sleep

It never rains.
Dust the colour of a faded rose buries you
and the home we built.
I do not mean the house.
Any fool can put clay and brick together
and occupy the walls he has raised.
I mean the flowers, that turned brown,
and the bushes that crumbled in the cold.
The fruit that, one season, never came back.

We put men on the moons
and launched the Ark, flung our empire
far enough to laugh at the Sun.
Feet from godhood, touching our lips
to the stars, to the young rock we picked out
already scarred by storms.

They never told us, but we knew.
Some descended, hunting for the Great Worm,
one final chance to rebuild
this place that we grew up in.
Others were like me, too old for prayer
and too disappointed in ourselves.

Now my years are collapsing into one another.
He is long gone, choked by the sand
billowing through his throat
that first year.
I know not the time of my death
but I know it will come soon;
I am the last. I must be the last.

The Ark will have spread its seed
on our new face now.
I think I will sleep tonight
and dream of when the dust was not so thick
on the grasses of the red hills
beneath the orange skyblooms at twilight.

– Roz Crowther

Roz Crowther is a Swansea-based writer with a strong interest in
science fiction. She also plays the bass guitar for various folk acts.

Ouroboros

                              bite
down with your oblong fangs,
grate into the notches bored in
your tail, a watch around
the world, counting time
eternally, concrete vertebrae
squeezing dust into being,
obsolete scales ringing out
mechanically, gagged cacophony
scraping rust from the rungs
of a crenellated tongue, brutal
cement tail crushed by the
gritted pillars of ouroboros'
bite

– Edmund Morton

Edmund Morton grew up in Slough and went to university in Aberystwyth, where his love of literature blossomed like one of Wordsworth's daffodils. He has previously performed his poetry at three of Aberystwyth's Poetry Slams (winning twice) and later helped to organise the event. His poetry has previously appeared in the anthology *Seafret*.

The Wait

The patio's centre doesn't match;
grey squares, edges decades-worn, marooned,
hemmed in by concrete thick with slate rafts
and daring green pushed by ants.
The wait really began here – discontinuity.
Thick white sweaty clouds.

We went to the cinema more again.
I returned to the sea, iron-heavy, pumped
by the heart of the moon.
My sister went back to the ancient colleges
and bicycle paths, cheese shops.
Calendars were crossed off back here.
Friends, unexpected ones too, drank coffee
and swapped survival stories.

The wait crept on, past the incisions
and removals, bandages and pills, phonecalls.
The wait counted off its time leisurely,
in fragile fingernails and red skin.
We rarely have guests at Christmas,
let alone nurses.

Five weeks of atomic jokes while hair re-grew,
baby-like, fuzz like a hamster or an Ikea cushion.
Five days a week taking a journey
the length of a Carry On film
up to Swansea, the nearest unit.

The wait fed itself on more than tick-tocks
and faces beaten clean by relentless hands.
It clamped inarticulate oncologists in its jaws,
swallowed doctors unable to act
like there was blood in their body.
The wait took the internet to the table
and cleaned its plate with crusts
of wrong sentences and shocked rambles.
But it could never gorge itself
on our fixed points, on your strength.

– George Sandifer-Smith

George Sandifer-Smith is a Welsh writer and postgraduate student at Aberystwyth University. He has self-published one novelette, *Pop Idle*, in 2013, and his first children's book, *Cholloo's Birthday*, was published by Lily Publications in 2014. He previously co-edited the 2014 poetry and fiction anthology, *Make Time for Aberystwyth*. His poetry has been published in magazines including the Cadaverine and Long Exposure Magazine.

How I know I need a biscuit in the afternoon

Getting lost in the curtains.
Being almost certain the cats are speaking

English or I am speaking cat.
A need for small spaces:

the airing cupboard, the fridge, a shoebox.
Shouting at the sofa's largesse.

Shutting the shouting in the airing cupboard.
Shoeboxing the sofa's ears.

Hoisting the curtains as sails for a ship
made from the fridge. Press-ganging

the cats for crew to haul anchor for the place
my neighbours whisper I'm bound

when they display their recycling
on Tuesdays. No, don't go –

have some custard creams and climb aboard.
There's always room for one more.

– Katherine Stansfield

Katherine Stansfield is a fiction writer, poet and reviewer. Her debut novel, *The Visitor* (Parthian, 2013), won the Hoyler an Gof Fiction Prize 2014. Her poems have been published in New Welsh Review, Poetry Wales, Poetry Cornwall, Planet, The Lampeter Review, and Magma. Her first collection of poems, *Playing House*, was published by Seren in October 2014. You can find her online at http://katherinestansfield.blogspot.co.uk/ and on Twitter (@k_stansfield).